A Year of Dishcloths

Popular designer Maggie Weldon invited her blog followers to participate in an amazing crochet project—365 dishcloths in a year. Yes, a dishcloth a day for the entire year of 2011! They embraced the challenge and began to submit their entries and compete for cash and prizes. Maggie and her team designed a large number of the cloths; our collection highlights the top 52, credited to the original designers in the challenge. We've categorized our dishcloths according to the season, and we know you'll find many designs that are perfect for your kitchen or gifts for all of your friends and family. Enjoy!

Spring Collection

Fall Collection

Summer Collection

Winter Collection

Table of Contents

Wild Rose

Design by Maggie Weldon

Skill Level

 EASY

Finished Measurement

10½ inches point to point

Materials

- Medium (worsted) weight cotton yarn:
  - 1 oz/50 yds/30g light green
  - ½ oz/25 yds/15g each white, dark green, light rose and dark rose

- Size I/9/5.5mm crochet hook
- Tapestry needle

Gauge

Gauge is not important for this project.

Pattern Notes

Weave in ends as work progresses.

Join with slip stitch as indicated unless otherwise stated.

Chain-3 at beginning of round counts as first double crochet unless otherwise stated.

Chain-6 at beginning of round counts as first double crochet and chain-3 unless otherwise stated.

Chain-5 at beginning of round counts as first half double crochet and chain-3 unless otherwise stated.

Special Stitch

Single crochet join (sc join): Place slip knot on hook, insert hook in indicated st, yo and draw up a lp, yo and draw through both lps on hook.

Dishcloth

Rnd 1 (RS): With dark rose, ch 5, sl st in first ch to form ring, ch 1, [sc, hdc, 2 dc, hdc] 6 times in ring, **join** (see Pattern Notes) in first sc. Fasten off dark rose. (6 petals)

Rnd 2: With RS facing, join light rose in any sc, ch 4, [sl st in next sc, ch 4] around, join in first sl st. (6 ch-4 lps)

Rnd 3: Sl st in next ch-4 lp, ch 1, (sc, hdc, 3 dc, hdc, sc) in same lp, (sc, hdc, 3 dc, hdc, sc) in each rem ch-4 lp around, join in first sc. (6 petals)

Rnd 4: Ch 1, sc in sp between first and last sc, working behind petals, ch 4, [sc in sp between next 2 sc, ch 4] around, join in first sc. (6 ch-4 lps)

Rnd 5: Ch 3, sl st in next sc on petal, working on rnd 3 of petals, [ch 3, sl st in next st] around, join in first sl st. Fasten off light rose.

Rnd 6: With RS facing, working behind petals, join dark green in any ch-4 lp on rnd 4, **ch 3** (see Pattern Notes), (2 dc, ch 2, 3 dc) in same lp, ch 1, [(3 dc, ch 2, 3 dc) in next ch-4 lp, ch 1] around, join in top of beg ch-3. Fasten off dark green. *(36 dc, 6 ch-2 sps, 6 ch-1 sps)*

Rnd 7: With RS facing, join white in any ch-2 sp, **ch 6** *(see Pattern Notes)*, dc in same sp, ch 1, sk next dc, dc in next dc, ch 1, dc in next ch-1 sp, ch 1, sk next dc, dc in next dc, ch 1, *(dc, ch 3, dc) in next ch-2 sp, ch 1, sk next dc, dc in next dc, ch 1, dc in next ch-1 sp, ch 1, sk next dc, dc in next dc, ch 1, rep from * around, join in 3rd ch of beg ch-6. Fasten off white. *(30 dc, 24 ch-1 sps, 6 ch-3 sps)*

Rnd 8: With RS facing, join light green in any corner ch-3 sp, ch 3, (dc, ch 3, 2 dc) in same sp, dc in next dc, [dc in next ch-1 sp, dc in next dc] 4 times, *(2 dc, ch 3, 2 dc) in next corner ch-3 sp, dc in next dc, [dc in next ch-1 sp, dc in next dc] 4 times, rep from * around, join in top of beg ch-3. Fasten off light green. *(78 dc, 4 ch-3 sps)*

Rnd 9: With RS facing, join white in any corner ch-3 sp, **ch 5** *(see Pattern Notes)*, hdc in same sp, [ch 1, sk next dc, hdc in next dc] 6 times, ch 1, sk next dc, *(hdc, ch 3, hdc) in next corner ch-3 sp, [ch 1, sk next dc, hdc in next dc] 6 times, ch 1, sk next dc, rep from * around, join in 2nd ch of beg ch-5. Fasten off white. *(48 hdc, 42 ch-1 sps, 6 ch-3 sps)*

Rnd 10: With RS facing, join light green in any corner ch-3 sp, ch 3, (dc, ch 2, 2 dc) in same sp, 2 dc in each of next 3 ch-1 sps, dc in next ch-1 sp, 2 dc in each of next 3 ch-1 sps, *(2 dc, ch 2, 2 dc) in next corner ch-3 sp, 2 dc in each of next 3 ch-1 sps, dc in next ch-1 sp, 2 dc in each of next 3 ch-1 sps, rep from * around, join in top of beg ch-3. Fasten off light green. *(102 dc, 6 ch-2 sps)*

Rnd 11: With RS facing, **sc join** *(see Special Stitch)* dark green in any corner ch-2 sp, ch 2, sc in same sp, ch 2, [sk next dc, sc in next dc, ch 2] around, working (sc, ch 2, sc) in each corner ch-2 sp, join in first sc. Fasten off. ●

Lacy Violets

Design by Maggie Weldon

Skill Level

 EASY

Finished Measurements

9 inches wide x 8 inches long

Materials
- Medium (worsted) weight cotton yarn:
    - 1½ oz/75 yds/45g white
    - ½ oz/25 yds/15g lilac
    - ¼ oz/13 yds/8g each green and purple
- Size H/8/5mm crochet hook
- Tapestry needle

4 MEDIUM

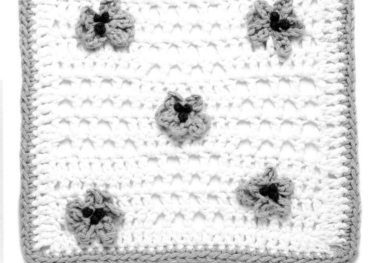

Gauge

Gauge is not important for this project.

Pattern Notes

Chain-3 at beginning of row or round counts as first double crochet unless otherwise stated.

Chain-4 at beginning of row counts as first double crochet and chain-1 unless otherwise stated.

Join with slip stitch as indicated unless otherwise stated.

Special Stitches

Shell: (2 dc, ch 2, 2 dc) in st as indicated in instructions.

Single crochet join (sc join): Place slip knot on hook, insert hook in indicated st, yo and draw up a lp, yo and draw through both lps on hook.

Dishcloth

Row 1 (RS): With white, ch 27, dc in 4th ch from hook *(sk chs count as first dc)*, dc in each of next 7 chs, [ch 1, sk next ch, dc in next ch] 4 times, dc in each of next 8 chs, turn. *(21 dc, 4 ch-1 sps)*

Row 2: Ch 3 *(see Pattern Notes)*, dc in each of next 8 dc, [ch 1, dc in next dc] 4 times, dc in each of next 8 dc, turn.

Rows 3 & 4: Rep row 2.

Row 5: Ch 4 *(see Pattern Notes)*, sk next dc, [dc in next dc, ch 1, sk next dc] 3 times, [dc in next dc, dc in next ch-1 sp] 4 times, dc in next dc, [ch 1, sk next dc, dc in next dc] 4 times, turn. *(17 dc, 8 ch-1 sps)*

Row 6: Ch 4, [dc in next dc, ch 1] 3 times, dc in each of next 9 dc, [ch 1, dc in next dc] 4 times, turn.

Rows 7 & 8: Rep row 6.

Row 9: Ch 3, [dc in next ch-1 sp, dc in next dc] 4 times, [ch 1, sk next dc, dc in next dc] 4 times, [dc in next ch-1 sp, dc in next dc] 4 times, turn.

Rows 10–12: Rep rows 2–4.

At the end of row 12, do not turn.

Edging

Rnd 1 (WS): Ch 3, (dc, ch 2, 2 dc) in last dc of row 12, working in row ends on side of Dishcloth, 2 dc in each row end across, working across opposite side of foundation ch, **shell** *(see Special Stitches)* in first ch, dc in each rem ch across to last ch, shell in last ch, working in row ends on opposite side of Dishcloth, 2 dc in each row end across, working across row 12, shell in first dc, dc in each dc and ch sp across, **join** *(see Pattern Notes)* in top of beg ch-3. Fasten off. *(108 dc)*

Rnd 2: With RS facing, **sc join** *(see Special Stitches)* lilac in any corner ch-2 sp, 2 sc in same sp, sc in each dc around, working 3 sc in each corner ch-2 sp, join in first sc. Fasten off.

Flower
Make 5.

With lilac, ch 6, sl st in first ch, [ch 5, sl st in first foundation ch] 4 times. Fasten off. *(5 petals)*

Leaf
Make 5.

With green, ch 8, sl st in first ch, ch 7, sl st in first foundation ch. Fasten off.

Finishing

With RS of Dishcloth facing, position Leaves and Flowers on solid blocks as shown in photo. Using purple and working through all thicknesses, attach Flowers and Leaves by embroidering 3 **french knots** *(see illustration)* in center of each Flower. ●

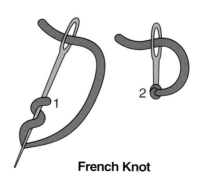

French Knot

Tulips

Design by Maggie Weldon

Skill Level

 EASY

Finished Measurement

8¾ inches in diameter

Materials

- Medium (worsted) weight cotton yarn:
  1 oz/50 yds/30g white
  ¼ oz/13 yds/8g each dark pink, light pink, yellow and green
- Size G/6/4mm crochet hook
- Tapestry needle

Gauge

Gauge is not important for this project.

Pattern Notes

Chain-3 at beginning of round counts as first double crochet unless otherwise stated.

Join with slip stitch as indicated unless otherwise stated.

Chain-2 at beginning of row counts as first half double crochet unless otherwise stated.

Chain-18 at beginning of Leaves and Stems counts as a chain-5 foundation chain and chain-13 of first Leaf.

Special Stitches

Single crochet join (sc join): Place slip knot on hook, insert hook in indicated st, yo and draw up a lp, yo and draw through both lps on hook.

Picot: Ch 3, sl st in 3rd ch from hook as indicated in instructions.

Dishcloth

Rnd 1 (RS): With white, ch 4, sl st in first ch to form ring, **ch 3** (see Pattern Notes), 11 dc in ring, **join** (see Pattern Notes) in top of beg ch-3. (12 dc)

Rnd 2: Ch 3, dc in same st as joining, 2 dc in each rem dc around, join in top of beg ch-3. (24 dc)

Rnd 3: Ch 3, dc in same st as joining, dc in next dc, [2 dc in next dc, dc in next dc] around, join in top of beg ch-3. (36 dc)

Rnd 4: Ch 3, dc in same st as joining, dc in each of next 2 dc, [2 dc in next dc, dc in each of next 2 dc] around, join in top of beg ch-3. (48 dc)

Rnd 5: Ch 3, dc in same st as joining, dc in each of next 3 dc, [2 dc in next dc, dc in each of next 3 dc] around, join in top of beg ch-3. (60 dc)

Rnd 6: Ch 3, dc in same st as joining, dc in each of next 4 dc, [2 dc in next dc, dc in each of next 4 dc] around, join in top of beg ch-3. Fasten off. (72 dc)

Rnd 7: With RS facing, **sc join** *(see Special Stitches)* dark pink in any dc, [ch 3, sk next dc, sc in next dc] around, ch 3, join in first sc. Fasten off. *(36 sc, 36 ch-3 sps)*

Flower
Make 1 each dark pink, light pink & yellow.

Row 1: Ch 3, (sc, hdc) in 3rd ch from hook, turn. *(3 sts)*

Row 2: Ch 2 *(see Pattern Notes)*, sc in first st, sc in next st, (sc, hdc) in last st, turn. *(5 sts)*

Rows 3–5: Ch 1, sc in each st across, turn.

Row 6: Ch 3, (3 hdc, sl st) in first sc, sc in next sc, (2 dc, **picot**—*see Special Stitches*, 2 dc) in next sc, sc in next sc, (sl st, ch 1, sc, 3 hdc, ch 3, sl st) in last sc, working in row ends along bottom of Flower, sc in each row end around to beg ch-3. Leaving long end for sewing, fasten off.

Leaves & Stem
With green, **ch 18** *(see Pattern Notes)*, sc in 2nd ch from hook and in each of next 11 chs *(first Leaf made)*, sl st in next ch, [ch 17, sl st in 2nd ch from hook and in each of next 15 chs, sl st in next ch on foundation ch *(Stem made)*] 3 times, ch 13, sc in 2nd ch from hook and in each of next 11 chs *(2nd Leaf made)*, sl st in last foundation ch, working across opposite side of foundation ch, sc in each ch across, join in first sc. Leaving long end for sewing, fasten off. *(2 Leaves, 3 Stems)*

Finishing
Using long ends and tapestry needle, sew Leaves and Stems to front of Dishcloth as shown in photo. Sew 1 Flower on top of each Stem. ●

Cornflower

Design by Carol Ballard

Skill Level
 EASY

Finished Measurement
9½ inches square

Materials
- Medium (worsted) weight cotton yarn:
  - 2 oz/100 yds/60g white
  - 1 oz/50 yds/30g blue
  - ½ oz/25 yds/15g dark green
- Size H/8/5mm crochet hook or size needed to obtain gauge
- Tapestry needle

4 MEDIUM

Gauge

6 dc = 2 inches; 3 dc rows = 2 inches

Take time to check gauge.

Pattern Notes

Join with slip stitch as indicated unless otherwise stated.

Chain-4 at beginning of round counts as first treble crochet unless otherwise stated.

Chain-3 at beginning of round counts as first double crochet unless otherwise stated.

Special Stitches

Beginning cluster (beg cl): Ch 2, holding last lp of each st on hook, 2 dc as indicated in instructions, yo, pull through all lps on hook.

Cluster (cl): Holding last lp of each st on hook, 3 dc as indicated in instructions, yo, pull through all lps on hook.

Single crochet join (sc join): Place slip knot on hook, insert hook in indicated st, yo and draw up a lp, yo and draw through both lps on hook.

Dishcloth

Rnd 1 (RS): With blue, ch 2, 8 sc in 2nd ch from hook, **join** *(see Pattern Notes)* in first sc. (8 sc)

Rnd 2: Ch 4 *(see Pattern Notes)*, 2 tr in same st as joining, 3 tr in each rem sc around, join in **front lp** *(see Stitch Guide)* of 4th ch of beg ch-4. *(24 tr)*

Rnd 3: Ch 1, working in front lps, (sc, ch 2, dc) in same st as joining, (sc, ch 2, dc) in each rem tr around, join in **back lp** *(see Stitch Guide)* of 4th ch of beg ch-4 on rnd 2. *(24 petals)*

Rnd 4: Ch 1, working in back lps on rnd 2, sc in same st as joining, sc in each of next 2 tr, 2 sc in next tr, [sc in each of next 3 tr, 2 sc in next tr] around, join in front lp of first sc. *(30 sc)*

Rnd 5: Ch 1, working in front lps on rnd 4, (sc, ch 2, dc) in same st as joining, (sc, ch 2, dc) in each rem sc around, join in back lp of first sc on rnd 4. Fasten off blue. *(30 petals)*

Rnd 6: With RS facing, join dark green in back lp of any sc on rnd 4, **ch 3** *(see Pattern Notes)*, dc in same st as joining, dc in each of next 2 sc, [2 dc in next sc, dc in each of next 2 sc] around, join in top of beg ch-3. *(40 dc)*

Rnd 7: Beg cl *(see Special Stitches)* in same st as joining, ch 3, **cl** *(see Special Stitches)* in same st, [ch 1, sk next dc, cl in next dc] 4 times, ch 1, *(cl, ch 3, cl) in next dc, [ch 1, sk next dc, cl in next dc] 4 times, ch 1, rep from * around, join in top of first cl. Fasten off dark green.

Rnd 8: With RS facing, join white in any corner ch-3 sp, ch 3, (2 dc, ch 1, 3 dc) in same sp, [dc in next cl, 2 dc in next ch-1 sp] 5 times, dc in next cl, *(3 dc, ch 1, 3 dc) in next corner ch-3 sp, [dc in next cl, 2 dc in next ch-1 sp] 5 times, dc in next cl, rep from * around, join in top of beg ch-3. *(84 dc, 4 ch-1 sps)*

Rnd 9: Ch 3, dc in each of next 2 dc, [(dc, ch 1, dc) in next ch-1 sp, dc in each of next 9 dc, **fpdc** *(see Stitch Guide)* around each of next 3 dc, dc in each of next 10 dc] 3 times, (dc, ch 1, dc) in next ch-1 sp, dc in each of next 9 dc, fpdc around each of next 3 dc, dc in each of next 7 dc, join in top of beg ch-3. *(80 dc, 4 ch-1 sps, 12 fpdc)*

Rnd 10: Ch 3, dc in each of next 3 dc, [(dc, ch 1, dc) in next ch-1 sp, dc in each of next 10 dc, fpdc around each of next 3 fpdc, dc in each of next 11 dc] 3 times, (dc, ch 1, dc) in next ch-1 sp, dc in each of next 10 dc, fpdc around each of next 3 fpdc, dc in each of next 7 dc, join in top of beg ch-3. Fasten off white. *(88 dc, 4 ch-1 sps, 12 fpdc)*

Edging

Rnd 1: With RS facing, **sc join** *(see Special Stitches)* blue in any corner ch-1 sp, 2 sc in same sp, sc in each dc around, working 3 sc in each corner ch-1 sp, join in first sc. Fasten off. ●

Passion Flower

Design by Debbie Franklin

Skill Level

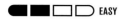 ◼︎◼︎☐☐ **EASY**

Finished Measurement

8 inches in diameter

Materials

- Medium (worsted) weight cotton yarn:
    2 oz/100 yds/60g purple
    1 oz/50 yds/30g white
- Size H/8/5mm crochet hook
- Tapestry needle
- Stitch marker
- Yellow nylon netting: ¼ yd

Gauge

Gauge is not important for this project.

Pattern Notes

Join with slip stitch as indicated unless otherwise stated.

Chain-5 at beginning of round counts as first double crochet and chain-2 space unless otherwise stated.

Chain-3 at beginning of round counts as first double crochet unless otherwise stated.

Flower Center is worked in continuous rounds; do not turn or join unless otherwise stated.

Mark first stitch of round.

Special Stitches

Small shell (sm shell): (2 dc, ch 2, 2 dc) in indicated st or sp.

Large shell (lg shell): (3 dc, ch 2, 3 dc) in indicated st or sp.

Dishcloth

Rnd 1 (RS): Beg at center with purple, ch 4, sl st in first ch to form ring, ch 1, 10 hdc in ring, **join** (see Pattern Notes) in first hdc. (10 hdc)

Rnd 2: Ch 1, 2 hdc in each hdc around, join in first hdc. (20 hdc)

Rnd 3: Ch 1, hdc in first hdc, 2 hdc in each rem hdc around, join in first hdc. (39 hdc)

Rnd 4: Ch 5 (see Pattern Notes), 2 dc in same st, *ch 1, sk next 2 hdc**, **sm shell** (see Special Stitches) in next dc, rep from * around, ending last rep at **, dc in same st as first st, join in 3rd ch of beg ch-5. (13 shells)

Rnd 5: Sl st in first ch-2 sp, ch 5, 2 dc in same sp, [ch 1, shell in ch-2 sp of next shell] around, ch 1, dc in first ch-2 sp, join in 3rd ch of beg ch-5.

Rnds 6 & 7: Sl st in first ch-2 sp, ch 5, 3 dc in same sp, [ch 1, **lg shell** (see Special Stitches) in ch-2 sp of next shell] around, ch 1, 2 dc in first ch-2 sp, join in 3rd ch of beg ch-5.

At end of rnd 7, fasten off purple.

Rnd 8: With RS facing, join white in ch-2 sp of any lg shell, **ch 3** *(see Pattern Notes)*, 7 dc in same ch-2 sp, [sc in next ch-1 sp, 8 dc in ch-2 sp of next lg shell] around, sc in next ch-1 sp, join in top of beg ch-3. *(13 8-dc groups)*

Rnd 9: Ch 1, *sc in each of next 8 dc, ch 1, sc in next ch-1 sp on rnd 7, ch 1, sc in next ch-1 sp on rnd 6, ch 1, sc in next ch-1 sp on rnd 5, 2 sc in next ch-1 sp on rnd 4, ch 1, sc in next ch-1 sp on rnd 5, ch 1, sc in next ch-1 sp on rnd 6, ch 1, sc in next ch-1 sp on rnd 7, ch 1, rep from * around, join in first sc. Fasten off.

Flower Center

Getting started: Cut nylon netting into 1-inch strips. Join strips tog to form 1 long strip.

Rnd 1 (RS): Starting at center with strip of nylon netting, ch 2, 6 sc in 2nd ch from hook, **do not join** *(see Pattern Notes)*. **Place marker in first st** *(see Pattern Notes)*. *(6 sc)*

Rnd 2: 2 sc in next sc and in each rem sc around. *(12 sc)*

Rnd 3: [2 sc in next sc, sc in next sc] around. *(18 sc)*

Rnd 4: [2 sc in next sc, sc in each of next 2 sc] around, join in next sc. Fasten off. *(24 sc)*

With RS facing, sew Flower Center to center of Dishcloth as pictured. ●

Peach Delight
Design by Maggie Weldon

Skill Level
 EASY

Finished Measurements
8½ inches wide x 8 inches long

Materials
- Medium (worsted) weight cotton yarn:
    1½ oz/75 yds/45g each off-white and peach variegated
    ½ oz/25 yds/15g yellow
- Size H/8/5mm crochet hook
- Tapestry needle

Gauge
Gauge is not important for this project.

Pattern Notes
Chain-3 at beginning of round counts as first double crochet unless otherwise stated.

Join with slip stitch as indicated unless otherwise stated.

Chain-8 at beginning of round counts as first double crochet and chain-5 space unless otherwise stated.

Special Stitches

Beginning shell (beg shell): Ch 3, (2 dc, ch 2, 3 dc) in indicated st or sp.

Shell: (3 dc, ch 2, 3 dc) in indicated st or sp.

Dishcloth

Rnd 1 (RS): Beg at center with yellow, ch 4, sl st in first ch to form ring, **ch 3** *(see Pattern Notes)*, 2 dc in ring, ch 2, [3 dc in ring, ch 2] 3 times, **join** *(see Pattern Notes)* in first dc. Fasten off yellow. *(12 dc, 4 ch-2 sps)*

Rnd 2: With RS facing, join off-white in any corner ch-2 sp, **beg shell** *(see Special Stitches)* in same sp, ch 1, [**shell** *(see Special Stitches)* in next ch-2 sp, ch 1] around, join in top of beg ch-3. *(4 shells, 4 ch-1 sps)*

Rnd 3: Sl st in each of next 2 dc, sl st in next ch-2 sp, beg shell in same sp, ch 1, 3 dc in next ch-1 sp, ch 1, [shell in next corner ch-2 sp, ch 1, 3 dc in next ch-1 sp, ch 1] around, join in top of beg ch-3.

Rnd 4: Sl st in each of next 2 dc, sl st in next ch-2 sp, beg shell in same sp, ch 1, [3 dc in next ch-1 sp, ch 1] twice, *shell in next corner ch-2 sp, ch 1, [3 dc in next ch-1 sp, ch 1] twice, rep from * around, join in top of beg ch-3.

Rnd 5: Sl st in each of next 2 dc, sl st in next ch-2 sp, beg shell in same sp, ch 1, [3 dc in next ch-1 sp, ch 1] 3 times, *shell in next corner ch-2 sp, ch 1, [3 dc in next ch-1 sp, ch 1] 3 times, rep from * around, join in top of beg ch-3. Fasten off off-white.

Rnd 6: With RS facing, join peach in any corner ch-2 sp, beg shell in same sp, ch 1, [3 dc in next ch-1 sp, ch 1] 4 times, *shell in next corner ch-2 sp, ch 1, [3 dc in next ch-1 sp, ch 1] 4 times, rep from * around, join in top of beg ch-3.

Rnd 7: Ch 1, sc in first dc, sc in each of next 2 dc, *(sc, ch 2, sc) in next corner ch-2 sp, [sc in each of next 3 dc, (sc, ch 2, sc) in next ch-1 sp] 5 times**, sc in next 3 dc, rep from * around, ending last rep at **, join in first sc. Fasten off.

Flower

Rnd 1: With RS facing, join peach around post of any dc on rnd 1 of Dishcloth, **ch 8** *(see Pattern Notes)*, [dc around post of next dc, ch 5] around, join in 3rd ch of beg ch-8. *(12 dc, 12 ch-5 lps)*

Rnd 2: Working in front of ch-5 lps on rnd 1 of Dishcloth, dc around post of same dc as joining, ch 3, [dc around post of next dc, ch 3] around, join in first dc. Fasten off. *(12 dc, 12 ch-3 lps)* ●

Daffodil

Design by Maggie Weldon

Skill Level

 EASY

Finished Measurement

8¾ inches in diameter

Materials

- Medium (worsted) weight cotton yarn:
  ½ oz/25 yds/15g each white, orange, dark yellow, light yellow and green
- Size G/6/4mm crochet hook
- Tapestry needle

Gauge

Gauge is not important for this project.

Pattern Notes

Weave in ends as work progresses.

Join with slip stitch as indicated unless otherwise stated.

Chain-2 at beginning of round counts as first half double crochet unless otherwise stated.

Chain-4 at beginning of round counts as first double crochet and chain-1 space unless otherwise stated.

Chain-3 at beginning of round counts as first double crochet unless otherwise stated.

Special Stitches

V-stitch (V-st): (Dc, ch 1, dc) in indicated st or sp.

Single crochet join (sc join): Place slip knot on hook, insert hook in indicated st, yo and draw up a lp, yo and draw through both lps on hook.

Dishcloth

Rnd 1 (RS): With orange, ch 4, sl st in first ch to form ring, ch 1, 8 sc in ring, **join** *(see Pattern Notes)* in first sc. Fasten off orange. *(8 sc)*

Rnd 2: With RS facing, join dark yellow in **front lp** *(see Stitch Guide)* of any sc, working in front lps, *ch 2, sl st in next sc, rep from * around, ch 2, join in first sl st. *(8 ch-2 sps)*

Rnd 3: (Sc, ch 2, sc) in each ch-2 sp around, join in first sc. Fasten off dark yellow.

Rnd 4: With RS facing, join light yellow in **back lp** *(see Stitch Guide)* of any sc on rnd 1, working behind rnds 2 and 3, *ch 4, sl st in back lp of next sc, rep from * around, ch 4, join in first sl st. *(8 ch-4 sps)*

Rnd 5: Sl st in next ch-4 sp, **ch 2** *(see Pattern Notes)*, (dc, 3 tr, dc, hdc) in same ch-4 sp, ch 1, *(hdc, dc, 3 tr, dc, hdc) in next ch-4 sp, ch 1, rep from * around, join in top of beg ch-2. *(8 petals)*

Rnd 6: Working behind petals, [ch 4, sl st in next ch-1 sp] 8 times. Fasten off light yellow. *(8 ch-4 sps)*

Rnd 7: With RS facing, join green in any ch-4 sp, **ch 4** *(see Pattern Notes)*, (dc, **V-st**—*see Special Stitches*) in same sp, [2 V-sts in next ch-4 sp] 7 times, join in 3rd ch of beg ch-4. Fasten off green. *(16 V-sts)*

Rnd 8: With RS facing, join white in any ch-1 sp, **ch 3** *(see Pattern Notes)*, 2 dc in same sp, 3 dc in each rem ch-1 sp around, join in top of beg ch-3. *(48 dc)*

Rnd 9: Ch 4, dc in same st as joining, sk next dc, [V-st in next dc, sk next dc] around, join in 3rd ch of beg ch-4. *(24 V-sts)*

Rnd 10: Ch 3, 2 dc in same st as joining, 3 dc in each rem ch-1 sp around, join in top of beg ch-3. Fasten off white. *(72 dc)*

Rnd 11: With RS facing, **sc join** *(see Special Stitches)* orange in any dc, ch 2, sc in same st, sk next dc, [(sc, ch 2, sc) in next dc, sk next dc] around, join in first sc. Fasten off. ●

Forget-Me-Not

Design by Maggie Weldon

Skill Level

⬤⬛◻️◻️ EASY

Finished Measurement

9½ inches in diameter

Materials

- Medium (worsted) weight cotton yarn:
  - 1½ oz/75 yds/45g white
  - ½ oz/25 yds/15g each light blue and green
- Size H/8/5mm crochet hook
- Tapestry needle

Gauge

Gauge is not important for this project.

Pattern Notes

Join with slip stitch as indicated unless otherwise stated.

Chain-3 at beginning of round counts as first double crochet unless otherwise stated.

Special Stitches

Cluster (cl): Holding last lp of each st on hook, 2 tr as indicated in instructions, yo, pull through all lps on hook.

Single crochet join (sc join): Place slip knot on hook, insert hook in indicated st, yo and draw up a lp, yo and draw through both lps on hook.

Dishcloth

Rnd 1 (RS): With blue, ch 4, sl st in first ch to form ring, [(ch 4, **cl**—*see Special Stitches*, ch 4, sl st) in ring] 5 times, (ch 4, cl, tr) in ring. *(6 petals)*

Rnd 2: [Ch 4, (sc, ch 2, sc) in next cl] around, **join** *(see Pattern Notes)* in first ch. Fasten off blue. *(6 ch-4 lps, 12 sc, 6 ch-2 sps)*

Rnd 3: With RS facing, **sc join** *(see Special Stitches)* green in any ch-4 lp, ch 6, sc in same lp, (2 dc, ch 3, 2 dc) in next ch-2 sp, [(sc, ch 6, sc) in next ch-4 lp, (2 dc, ch 3, 2 dc) in next ch-2 sp] around, join in first sc. Fasten off green. *(12 sc, 6 ch-6 lps, 24 dc, 6 ch-3 sps)*

Rnd 4: With RS facing, sc join white in any ch-3 sp, ch 6, sc in next ch-6 lp, ch 6, [sc in next ch-3 sp, ch 6, sc in next ch-6 lp, ch 6] around, join in first sc. *(12 sc, 12 ch-6 lps)*

Rnd 5: Sl st in first ch-6 lp, **ch 3** *(see Pattern Notes)*, (2 dc, ch 2, 3 dc) in same lp, sl st in next sc, [(3 dc, ch 2, 3 dc) in next ch-6 lp, sl st in next sc] around, join in top of beg ch-3. *(72 dc, 12 ch-2 sps, 12 sl sts)*

Rnd 6: Sl st in next dc, ch 3, dc in next dc, (2 dc, ch 3, 2 dc) in next ch-2 sp, dc in each of next 2 dc, sk next dc, sk next sl st, sk next dc, [dc in each of next 2 dc, (2 dc, ch 3, 2 dc) in next ch-2 sp, dc in each of next 2 dc, sk next dc, sk next sl st, sk next dc] around, join in top of beg ch-3. *(96 dc, 12 ch-3 sps)*

Rnd 7: Sl st in next dc, ch 3, dc in each of next 2 dc, (2 dc, ch 2, 2 dc) in next ch-2 sp, dc in each of next 3 dc, sk next 2 dc, [dc in each of next 3 dc, (2 dc, ch 2, 2 dc) in next ch-2 sp, dc in each of next 3 dc, sk next 2 dc] around, join in top of beg ch-3. Fasten off. *(120 dc, 12 ch-2 sps)* ●

Grandmother's Flower Garden

Design by Maggie Weldon

Skill Level

 EASY

Finished Measurement

8¾ inches in diameter

Materials

- Medium (worsted) weight cotton yarn:
    - 1½ oz/75 yds/45g purple
    - 1 oz/50 yds/30g each yellow and beige
- Size H/8/5mm crochet hook
- Tapestry needle

4 MEDIUM

Gauge

Gauge is not important for this project.

Pattern Notes

Chain-4 at beginning of round counts as first double crochet and chain-1 unless otherwise stated.

Join with slip stitch as indicated unless otherwise stated.

Chain-3 at beginning of round counts as first double crochet unless otherwise stated.

Special Stitch

Single crochet join (sc join): Place slip knot on hook, insert hook in indicated st, yo and draw up a lp, yo and draw through both lps on hook.

Dishcloth

Motif
Make 1 yellow & 6 purple.

Rnd 1 (RS): Ch 4, sl st in first ch to form ring, **ch 4** *(see Pattern Notes)*, [(dc, ch 1) in ring] 11 times, **join** *(see Pattern Notes)* in 3rd ch of beg ch-4. *(12 dc, 12 ch-1 sps)*

Rnd 2: Sl st in same sp as previous join, **ch 3** *(see Pattern Notes)*, (dc, ch 2, 2 dc) in same sp, dc in next ch-1 sp, *(2 dc, ch 2, 2 dc) in next ch-1 sp, dc in next ch-1 sp, rep from * around, join in top of beg ch-3. Leaving long end for sewing, fasten off. *(30 dc, 6 ch-2 sps)*

Sew purple Motifs around yellow Motif as shown in photo. Sew adjacent sides of all Motifs tog.

Edging
Rnd 1: With RS facing, **sc join** *(see Special Stitch)* beige in ch-2 sp to left of any join, *[sc in each of next 4 dc,

3 sc in next ch-2 sp] twice, sc in each of next 4 dc**, sc in each of next 2 ch-2 sps, rep from * around, ending last rep at **, sc in last ch-2 sp, join in first sc. *(20 sc on each petal—120 sc total)*

Rnd 2: Sl st in next sc, ch 3, dc in next sc, hdc in each of next 2 sc, sc in each of next 10 sc, hdc in each of next 2 sc, dc in each of next 2 sc, sk next 2 sc, *dc in each of next 2 sc, hdc in each of next 2 sc, sc in each of next 10 sc, hdc in each of next 2 sc, dc in each of next 2 sc, sk next 2 sc, rep from * around, join in top of beg ch-3. Fasten off. ●

Thirteen Grannies in a Square

Design by Maggie Weldon

Skill Level
 **EASY**

Finished Measurement
9 inches square

Materials
- Medium (worsted) weight cotton yarn:
  1½ oz/75 yds/45g each pink and white fleck
- Size H/8/5mm crochet hook
- Tapestry needle

Gauge
Gauge is not important for this project.

Pattern Notes
Chain-5 at beginning of round counts as first double

crochet and chain-2 unless otherwise stated.

Join with slip stitch as indicated unless otherwise stated.

Chain-3 at beginning of round counts as first double crochet unless otherwise stated.

Special Stitch

Single crochet join (sc join): Place slip knot on hook, insert hook in indicated st, yo and draw up a lp, yo and draw through both lps on hook.

Dishcloth

Center Motif

Rnd 1 (RS): With white fleck, ch 6, sl st in first ch to form ring, **ch 5** *(see Pattern Notes)*, [4 dc in ring, ch 2] 3 times, 3 dc in ring, **join** *(see Pattern Notes)* in 3rd ch of beg ch-5. *(16 dc, 4 corner ch-2 sps)*

Rnd 2: Sl st in first ch-2 sp, ch 5, 2 dc in same sp, dc in next dc and in each rem dc across to next corner, *(2 dc, ch 2, 2 dc) in corner ch-2 sp, dc in next dc and in each rem dc across to next corner, rep from * around, dc in first corner ch-2 sp, join in 3rd ch of beg ch-5. *(32 dc, 4 corner ch-2 sps)*

Rnd 3: Rep rnd 2. Fasten off. *(48 dc, 4 corner ch-2 sps)*

Small Motif

Make 12.

Rnd 1 (RS): With pink, ch 6, sl st in first ch to form ring, **ch 3** *(see Pattern Notes)*, 3 dc in ring, ch 2, [4 dc in ring, ch 2] 3 times, join in top of beg ch-3. Leaving long end for sewing, fasten off. *(16 dc, 4 corner ch-2 sps)*

Finishing

With RS facing and using long ends and yarn needle, sew Small Motifs around Center Motif as shown in photo. Sew adjacent sides of Small Motifs tog.

Border

Rnd 1: With RS facing and working around outer edge of Small Motifs, join white fleck in any corner ch-2 sp, ch 3, (dc, ch 2, 2 dc) in same sp, dc in each of next 4 dc, [dc in each of next 2 ch-2 sps, dc in each of next 4 dc] 3 times, *(2 dc, ch 2, 2 dc) in corner ch-2 sp, dc in each of next 4 dc, [dc in each of next 2 ch-2 sps, dc in each of next 4 dc] 3 times, rep from * around, join in top of beg ch-3.

Rnd 2: Ch 1, sc in same st as joining, sc in next dc and in each rem dc around, working (sc, ch 2, sc) in each corner ch-2 sp, join in first sc. Fasten off.

Rnd 3: With RS facing, **sc join** *(see Special Stitch)* pink in any corner ch-2 sp, ch 2, sc in same sp, sc in next sc and in each rem sc around, working (sc, ch 2, sc) in each corner ch-2 sp, join in first sc. Fasten off. ●

Morning Glories

Design by Maggie Weldon

Skill Level

 EASY

Finished Measurement

8¾ inches in diameter

Materials

- Medium (worsted) weight cotton yarn:
  1 oz/50 yds/30g white
  ½ oz/25 yds/15g dark blue
  ¼ oz/13 yds/8g each light blue and green
- Size G/6/4mm crochet hook
- Tapestry needle

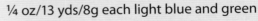

Gauge

Gauge is not important for this project.

Pattern Notes

Chain-3 at beginning of row or round counts as first double crochet unless otherwise stated.

Join with slip stitch as indicated unless otherwise stated.

Dishcloth

Rnd 1 (RS): With white, ch 4, sl st in first ch to form ring, **ch 3** *(see Pattern Notes)*, 11 dc in ring, **join** *(see Pattern Notes)* in top of beg ch-3. *(12 dc)*

Rnd 2: Ch 3, dc in same st as joining, 2 dc in each rem dc around, join in top of beg ch-3. *(24 dc)*

Rnd 3: Ch 3, dc in same st as joining, dc in next dc, [2 dc in next dc, dc in next dc] around, join in top of beg ch-3. *(36 dc)*

Rnd 4: Ch 3, dc in same st as joining, dc in each of next 2 dc, [2 dc in next dc, dc in each of next 2 dc] around, join in top of beg ch-3. *(48 dc)*

Rnd 5: Ch 3, dc in same st as joining, dc in each of next 3 dc, [2 dc in next dc, dc in each of next 3 dc] around, join in top of beg ch-3. *(60 dc)*

Rnd 6: Ch 3, dc in same st as joining, dc in each of next 4 dc, [2 dc in next dc, dc in each of next 4 dc] around, join in top of beg ch-3. Fasten off. *(72 dc)*

Rnd 7: With RS facing, join dark blue in any dc, ch 1, (sc, ch 1, sc) in same dc, ch 2, sk next 2 dc, *(sc, ch 1, sc) in next dc, ch 2, sk next 2 dc, rep from * around, join in first sc. Fasten off. *(48 sc, 24 ch-1 sps, 24 ch-2 sps)*

Flower

Make 1 each dark blue & light blue.

Row 1: Ch 4, 2 dc in 4th ch from hook *(sk chs count as first dc)*, turn. *(3 dc)*

Row 2: Ch 3, dc in first dc, dc in each rem dc across, turn. *(4 dc)*

Rows 3 & 4: Rep row 2. At end of row 4, ch 6, join in top of beg ch-3. *(6 dc at end of row 4)*

Rnd 5: Now working in rnds, ch 3, dc in same st as joining, 2 dc in each ch and dc around, join in top of beg ch-3. *(24 dc)*

Rnd 6: Ch 2, sl st in same st as joining, ch 2, sk next 2 dc, *(sl st, ch 2, sl st) in next dc, ch 2, sk next 2 dc, rep from * around, join in first sl st. Leaving long end for sewing, fasten off.

With white, sew lines on front of Flower as shown in photo.

Leaf With Vine

With green, ch 8, 2 dc in 3rd ch from hook, dc in next ch, 2 tr in next ch, dc in next ch, sc in next ch, (sl st, ch 1, sl st) in last ch, working across opposite side of foundation ch, sc in next ch, dc in next ch, 2 tr in next ch, dc in next ch, (2 dc, ch 2, sl st) in last ch, ch 12 *(for Vine)*, 2 sc in 2nd ch from hook and in each rem ch across. Leaving long end for sewing, fasten off.

Finishing

Using long ends and tapestry needle, sew Flowers and Leaf to front of Dishcloth as shown in photo. ●

Rose Granny

Design by Maggie Weldon

Skill Level

 EASY

Finished Measurement

9 inches square

Materials

- Medium (worsted) weight cotton yarn:
  - 1½ oz/75 yds/45g light blue
  - ½ oz/25 yds/15g white
  - ¼ oz/13 yds/8g each pink and green
- Size H/8/5mm crochet hook
- Tapestry needle

4 MEDIUM

Gauge

Gauge is not important for this project.

Pattern Notes

Chain-5 at beginning of round counts as first double crochet and chain-2 unless otherwise stated.

Join with slip stitch as indicated unless otherwise stated.

Special Stitch

Single crochet join (sc join): Place slip knot on hook, insert hook in indicated st, yo and draw up a lp, yo and draw through both lps on hook.

Dishcloth

Rnd 1 (RS): With blue, ch 4, sl st in first ch to form ring, **ch 5** *(see Pattern Notes)*, [(3 dc, ch 2) in ring] 3 times, 2 dc in ring, **join** *(see Pattern Notes)* in 3rd ch of beg ch-5. *(12 dc, 4 ch-2 sps)*

Rnd 2: Sl st in next ch-2 sp, ch 5, 3 dc in same sp, ch 1, [(3 dc, ch 2, 3 dc) in next ch-2 sp, ch 1] 3 times, 2 dc in first ch-2 sp, join in 3rd ch of beg ch-5. *(24 dc, 4 ch-2 sps)*

Rnd 3: Sl st in next ch-2 sp, ch 5, 3 dc in same sp, ch 1, 3 dc in next ch-1 sp, ch 1, [(3 dc, ch 2, 3 dc) in next corner ch-2 sp, ch 1, 3 dc in next ch-1 sp, ch 1] 3 times, 2 dc in first ch-2 sp, join in 3rd ch of beg ch-5. *(36 dc, 4 ch-2 sps)*

Rnd 4: Sl st in next ch-2 sp, ch 5, 3 dc in same sp, ch 1, (3 dc, ch 1) in each ch-1 sp across to next corner, *(3 dc, ch 2, 3 dc) in next corner ch-2 sp, ch 1, (3 dc, ch 1) in each ch-1 sp across to next corner, rep from * twice, 2 dc in first ch-2 sp, join in 3rd ch of beg ch-5. *(48 dc, 4 ch-2 sps)*

Rnds 5–7: Rep rnd 4. At end of rnd 7, fasten off. *(84 dc, 4 ch-2 sps)*

Outer Edging

Rnd 1: With RS facing, **sc join** (see Special Stitch) white in any corner ch-2 sp, ch 2, sc in same sp, *sk next dc, (sc, ch 2, sc) in next dc, [ch 3, sc in center dc of next 3-dc group on rnd 6, ch 3, (sc, ch 2, sc) in center dc of next 3-dc group on rnd 7] 6 times**, (sc, ch 2, sc) in next corner ch-2 sp, rep from * around, ending last rep at **, join in first sc. Fasten off.

Inner Edging

Rnd 1: With RS facing, sc join white in any corner ch-2 sp on rnd 3, ch 2, sc in same sp, *sk next dc, (sc, ch 2, sc) in next dc, [ch 3, sc in center dc of next 3-dc group on rnd 2, ch 3, (sc, ch 2, sc) in center dc of next 3-dc group on rnd 3] twice**, (sc, ch 2, sc) in next corner sp, rep from * around, ending last rep at **, join in first sc. Fasten off.

Rose

With pink, ch 7, (4 sc, sl st) in 2nd ch from hook and in each rem ch across. Leaving long end for sewing, fasten off. *(6 petals)*

Leaf Ring

With green, ch 11, sl st in first ch, [ch 10, sl st in first foundation ch] 4 times. Leaving long end for sewing, fasten off. *(5 leaves)*

Finishing

Using long end and tapestry needle, sew Rose to center of Leaf Ring. Sew Leaf Ring to center of Dishcloth as shown in photo. ●

Easter Bunny

Design by Carol Ballard

Skill Level

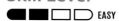 EASY

Finished Measurements

8¼ inches wide x 12 inches long, excluding Bow

Materials

- Medium (worsted) weight cotton yarn:
    2 oz/100 yds/60g white
    ¼ oz/13 yds/8g pink/blue/green variegated
- Size H/8/5mm crochet hook or size needed to obtain gauge
- Tapestry needle
- Embroidery needle
- Blue embroidery floss
- Pink embroidery floss

Gauge

3 sc = 1 inch; 4 rows = 1 inch

Take time to check gauge.

Pattern Notes

Do not work in stitch directly behind front post double crochet or back post double crochet unless otherwise stated.

Join with slip stitch as indicated unless otherwise stated.

Special Stitch

Long double crochet (long dc): Yo, insert hook in sc two rows below current working row, pull up lp to height of current working row, [yo, draw through 2 lps on hook] twice.

Dishcloth

Bunny

Row 1 (RS): With white, ch 23, sc in 2nd ch from hook and in each rem ch across, turn. *(22 sc)*

Row 2: Ch 1, 2 sc in first sc, sc in each rem sc across to last sc, 2 sc in last sc, turn. *(24 sc)*

Row 3: Ch 1, sc in each sc across, turn.

Row 4: Rep row 2. *(26 sc)*

Row 5: Rep row 3.

Row 6: Rep row 2. *(28 sc)*

Rows 7–10: [Rep row 3] 4 times.

Row 11: Ch 1, **sc dec** *(see Stitch Guide)*, sc in each rem sc across to last 2 sc, sc dec in last 2 sc, turn. *(26 sc)*

Rows 12 & 13: [Rep row 3] twice.

Row 14: Rep row 11. *(24 sc)*

Rows 15 & 16: [Rep row 3] twice.

Row 17: Rep row 11. *(22 sc)*

Rows 18–21: [Rep row 3] 4 times.

Row 22: Ch 2, sc in 2nd ch from hook, sc in first sc, **long dc** *(see Special Stitch)* in next sc, sc in each of next 18 sc, long dc in next sc, sc in last sc, turn. *(23 sts)*

Row 23: Ch 2, sc in 2nd ch from hook, sc in first sc, **fpdc** *(see Stitch Guide and Pattern Notes)* around next dc, sc in same dc, sc in each of next 18 sc, sc in next dc, fpdc around same dc, sc in each of next 2 sc, turn. *(26 sts)*

Row 24: Ch 1, sc in each of first 2 sc, sc in next fpdc, **bpdc** *(see Stitch Guide and Pattern Notes)* around same fpdc, sc in each of next 20 sc, bpdc around next fpdc, sc in same fpdc, sc in each of next 2 sc, turn. *(28 sts)*

Row 25: Ch 1, sc in each of first 3 sc, fpdc around next bpdc, sc in each of next 20 sc, fpdc around next bpdc, sc in each of next 3 sc, turn. *(28 sts)*

Row 26: Ch 1, sc in each of first 3 sc, bpdc around next fpdc, sc dec in next 2 sts, sc in each of next 16 sc, sc dec in next 2 sts, bpdc around next fpdc, sc in each of next 3 sc, turn. *(26 sts)*

Row 27: Ch 1, sc in each of first 3 sc, fpdc around next bpdc, sc dec in next 2 sts, sc in each of next 14 sc, sc dec in next 2 sts, fpdc around next bpdc, sc in each of next 3 sc, turn. *(24 sts)*

Row 28: Ch 1, sc in each of first 3 sc, bpdc around next fpdc, sc dec in next 2 sts, sc in each of next 12 sc, sc dec in next 2 sts, bpdc around next fpdc, sc in each of next 3 sc, turn. *(22 sts)*

Row 29: Ch 1, sc in each of first 3 sc, fpdc around next bpdc, sc in each of next 14 sc, fpdc around next bpdc, sc in each of next 3 sc, turn.

Row 30: Ch 1, sc in each of first 3 sc, bpdc around next fpdc, 2 sc in next sc, sc in each of next 12 sc, 2 sc in next sc, bpdc around next fpdc, sc in each of next 3 sc, turn. *(24 sts)*

Row 31: Ch 1, sc in each of first 3 sc, fpdc around next bpdc, sc in each of next 16 sc, fpdc around next bpdc, sc in each of next 3 sc, turn.

Row 32: Ch 1, sc in each of first 3 sc, bpdc around next fpdc, 2 sc in next sc, sc in each of next 14 sc, 2 sc in next sc, bpdc around next fpdc, sc in each of next 3 sc, turn. *(26 sts)*

Row 33: Ch 1, sc dec in first 2 sc, sc in next sc, fpdc around next bpdc, sc in each of next 18 sc, fpdc around next bpdc, sc in next sc, sc dec in last 2 sc, turn. *(24 sts)*

Row 34: Ch 1, sc in each of first 2 sts, bpdc around next fpdc, sc dec in next 2 sc, sc in each of next 14 sc, sc dec in next 2 sc, bpdc around next fpdc, sc in next 2 sts, turn. *(22 sts)*

Row 35: Ch 1, sc in each of first 2 sc, fpdc around next bpdc, sc dec in next 2 sts, sc in each of next 12 sc, sc dec in next 2 sts, fpdc around next bpdc, sc in each of next 2 sc, turn. *(20 sts)*

Row 36: Ch 1, sc in each of first 2 sc, bpdc around next fpdc, sc dec in next 2 sts, sc in each of next 10 sc, sc dec in next 2 sts, bpdc around next fpdc, sc in each of next 2 sc, turn. *(18 sts)*

Row 37: Ch 1, sc in each of first 2 sc, fpdc around next bpdc, sc dec in next 2 sts, sc in each of next 8 sc, sc dec in next 2 sts, fpdc around next bpdc, sc in each of next 2 sc, turn. *(16 sts)*

Row 38: Ch 1, sc dec in next 2 sc, bpdc around next fpdc, sc dec in next 2 sts, sc in each of next 6 sc, sc dec in next 2 sts, bpdc around next fpdc, sc dec in last 2 sc, turn. *(12 sts)*

Row 39: Ch 1, sc in first st, fpdc around next bpdc, sc dec in next 2 sts, sc in each of next 4 sc, sc dec in next 2 sts, fpdc around next bpdc, sc in last st, turn. *(10 sts)*

Row 40: Ch 1, sc dec in first 2 sts, sc in each of next 6 sc, sc dec in last 2 sts, turn. *(8 sc)*

Edging
Rnd 1: With RS facing, ch 1, sc in each sc and row end around entire piece, **join** *(see Pattern Notes)* in first sc. Fasten off.

Bow
Make 2.

Row 1 (RS): With variegated, ch 7, sc in 2nd ch from hook and in each rem ch across, turn. *(6 sc)*

Row 2: Ch 1, sc dec in first 2 sc, sc in each of next 2 sc, sc dec in last 2 sc, turn. *(4 sts)*

Row 3: Ch 1, sc dec in first 2 sts, sc dec in last 2 sts, turn. *(2 sts)*

Row 4: Ch 1, sc dec in first 2 sts, turn. *(1 st)*

Row 5: Ch 1, 2 sc in first st, turn. *(2 sc)*

Row 6: Ch 1, 2 sc in first sc, 2 sc in next sc, turn. *(4 sc)*

Row 7: Ch 1, 2 sc in first sc, sc in each of next 2 sc, 2 sc in last sc. *(6 sc)*

Edging
Rnd 1: With RS facing, sc evenly around entire Bow, join in first sc. Leaving long end for sewing, fasten off.

Finishing
With long ends, sew Bows on RS of Dishcloth as shown in photo.

With 2 strands variegated held tog and using **outline stitch** *(see illustration)*, embroider necklace on Bunny as shown in photo.

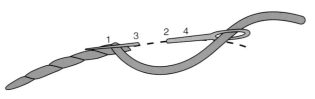

Outline Stitch

With embroidery needle and blue embroidery thread, using **satin stitch** and **backstitch** *(see illustrations),* embroider eyes on Bunny as shown in photo.

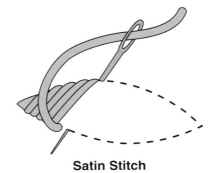

Satin Stitch

With embroidery needle and pink embroidery thread, using backstitch, embroider mouth on Bunny as shown in photo. ●

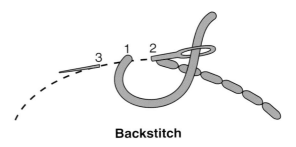

Backstitch

Shamrock

Design by Maggie Weldon

Skill Level
 EASY

Finished Measurement
9 inches square

Materials
- Medium (worsted) weight cotton yarn:
  1½ oz/75 yds/45g white
  1 oz/50 yds/30g light green
  ½ oz/25 yds/15g dark green
- Size H/8/5mm crochet hook
- Tapestry needle
- Dark green embroidery floss

Gauge
Gauge is not important for this project.

Pattern Note
Join with slip stitch as indicated unless otherwise stated.

Special Stitch

Single crochet join (sc join): Place slip knot on hook, insert hook in indicated st, yo and draw up a lp, yo and draw through both lps on hook.

Dishcloth

Row 1 (RS): With white, ch 24, sc in 2nd ch from hook and in each rem ch across, turn. *(23 sc)*

Rows 2–4: Ch 1, sc in each sc across, turn.

Rows 5–23: Referring to Color Chart, ch 1, sc in each sc across, turn.

COLOR KEY
☐ White
■ Light green

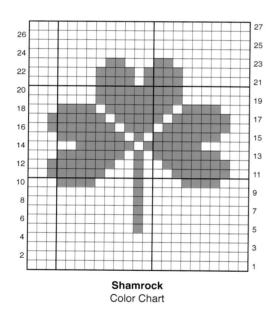

Shamrock
Color Chart

Rows 24–27: Ch 1, sc in each sc across, turn.

At end of row 27, fasten off.

Edging

Rnd 1: With RS facing, **sc join** *(see Special Stitch)* light green in first sc on last row, 2 sc in same sc, sc in each rem sc across to last sc, 3 sc in last sc, working in row ends along side of piece, sc evenly across to next corner, working across opposite side of foundation ch, 3 sc in first ch, sc in each rem ch across to last ch, 3 sc in last ch, working in row ends along opposite side, sc evenly across, **join** *(see Pattern Note)* in first sc. Fasten off.

Rnd 2: With RS facing, sc join white in any sc, sc in each rem sc around, working 3 sc in center sc of each corner 3-sc group, join in first sc. Fasten off.

Rnd 3: With RS facing, join dark green in any sc, ch 1, hdc in each sc around, working 4 hdc in center sc of each corner 3-sc group, join in first hdc. Fasten off.

Finishing

With dark green embroidery floss and using **backstitch** *(see illustration)*, outline leaves and stem on shamrock. ●

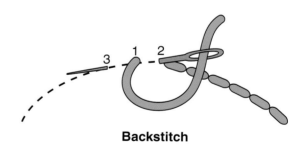

Backstitch

Summer Rose

Design by Maggie Weldon

Skill Level

 EASY

Finished Measurement

7½ inches square

Materials

- Medium (worsted) weight cotton yarn:
  1½ oz/75 yds/45g orange
  ½ oz/25 yds/15g each yellow and green
- Size H/8/5mm crochet hook
- Tapestry needle

4 MEDIUM

Gauge

Gauge is not important for this project.

Pattern Notes

Join with slip stitch as indicated unless otherwise stated.

Chain-3 at beginning of round counts as first double crochet unless otherwise stated.

Chain-4 at beginning of round counts as first double crochet and chain-1 unless otherwise stated.

Special Stitches

Beginning popcorn (beg pc): Ch 3, 3 dc as indicated in instructions, drop lp from hook, insert hook from front to back in top of ch-3, pick up dropped lp, draw through st.

Popcorn (pc): 4 dc as indicated in instructions, drop lp from hook, insert hook from front to back in top of ch-3, pick up dropped lp, draw through st.

Dishcloth

Rnd 1 (RS): With yellow, ch 6, sl st in first ch to form ring, **beg pc** *(see Special Stitches)* in ring, ch 2, [**pc** *(see Special Stitches)* in ring, ch 2] 7 times, **join** *(see Pattern Notes)* in top of first pc. *(8 pc, 8 ch-2 sps)*

Rnd 2: Sl st in next ch-2 sp, ch 1, (sc, ch 3, sc) in same sp, ch 3, [(sc, ch 3, sc) in next ch-sp 2, ch 3] around, join in first sc. Fasten off. *(16 sc, 16 ch-3 sps)*

Rnd 3: With RS facing, join green in first ch-3 sp, **ch 3** *(see Pattern Notes)*, (2 dc, ch 2, 3 dc) in same sp, ch 3, sk next ch-3 sp, sc in next ch-3 sp, ch 3, sk next ch-3 sp, [(3 dc, ch 2, 3 dc) in next ch-3 sp, ch 3, sk next ch-3 sp, sc in next ch-3 sp, ch 3, sk next ch-3 sp] around, join in top of beg ch-3. Fasten off. *(24 dc, 4 sc, 8 ch-3 sps, 4 ch-2 sps)*

Rnd 4: With RS facing, join orange in any corner ch-2 sp, ch 3, (2 dc, ch 2, 3 dc) in same sp, 3 dc in next ch-3 sp, ch 1, 3 dc in next ch-3 sp, [(3 dc, ch 2, 3 dc) in next corner ch-2 sp, 3 dc in next ch-3 sp, ch 1, 3 dc in next

(48 dc, 4 ch-1

otes), sk next
: corner ch-2
, ch 1, sk
3 times, rep

from * around, ending last rep at **, [dc in next dc, ch 1, sk next dc] twice, join in **back lp** *(see Stitch Guide)* of 3rd ch of beg ch-4. *(40 dc, 4 ch-2 sps, 36 ch-1 sps)*

Rnd 6: Ch 3, working in back lps, dc in each dc and ch around, working (2 dc, ch 2, 2 dc) in each corner ch-2 sp, join in top of beg ch-3. Fasten off. ●

mer Shells

sign by Maggie Weldon

Skill Level
■■□□ EASY

Finished Measurements
9 inches wide x 9½ inches tall

Materials
- Medium (worsted) weight cotton yarn:
  ½ oz/25 yds/15g each orange, yellow and green
- Size H/8/5mm crochet hook
- Tapestry needle

4 MEDIUM

Gauge
Gauge is not important for this project.

Pattern Notes
Weave in ends as work progresses.

Join with slip stitch as indicated unless otherwise stated.

Chain-3 at beginning of row counts as first double crochet unless otherwise stated.

Special Stitches
Shell: 5 dc as indicated in instructions.

Single crochet join (sc join): Place slip knot on

hook, insert hook in indicated st, yo and draw up a lp, yo and draw through both lps on hook.

Dishcloth
Row 1 (RS): With orange, ch 27, sc in 2nd ch from hook, sk next 2 chs, **shell** *(see Special Stitches)* in next ch, [sk next 4 chs, shell in next ch] 4 times, sk next 2 chs, sc in last ch. Fasten off orange. *(5 shells, 2 sc)*

Row 2: With RS facing, **join** *(see Pattern Notes)* yellow in first sc, **ch 3** *(see Pattern Notes)*, 2 dc in same sc, [sk next shell, sk next ch, working in front of last row, shell in next ch, sk next 2 chs] 4 times, sk next shell, 3 dc in last sc. Fasten off yellow. *(4 shells, 2 half shells)*

Row 3: With RS facing, **sc join** *(see Special Stitches)* green in first dc, ch 3, [working in front of last row, shell in center dc of next shell 2 rows below, sk next shell] 5 times, sc in last dc. Fasten off green. *(5 shells, 2 sc)*

Row 4: With RS facing, join orange in first sc, ch 3, 2 dc in same sc, [sk next shell, shell in center dc of next shell 2 rows below, sk next shell] 4 times, sk next shell, 3 dc in last sc. Fasten off orange. *(4 shells, 2 half shells)*

Row 5: With yellow, rep row 3.

Row 6: With green, rep row 4.

Row 7: With orange, rep row 3.

Row 8: With yellow, rep row 4.

Rows 9–20: [Rep rows 3–8 consecutively] twice.

At end row 20, fasten off.

Edging

Rnd 1: With RS facing, sc join green in first dc of last row, 2 sc in same dc, [hdc in next dc, sk next dc, working over last row, dc in center dc of next shell 2 rows below, hdc in next dc, sc in each of next 2 dc] across, working 3 sc in last st, working in row ends along side, sc in last row end, sc in next row end, [2 sc in next row end, sc in next row end] across, working across opposite side of foundation ch, 3 sc in first ch, sc in next ch-sp, [sc in next ch, 2 sc in next ch-sp, sc in next ch, sc in next ch-sp] 4 times, sc in next ch, sc in next ch-sp, 3 sc in last ch, working in row ends along opposite side, [2 sc in next row end, sc in next row end] across, join in first sc.

Rnd 2: Ch 1, sc in first sc, 2 sc in next sc, sc in each rem sc around, working 2 sc in each corner sc, join in first sc. Fasten off. ●

Bayberry

Design by Maggie Weldon

Skill Level
 INTERMEDIATE

Finished Measurements
8 inches wide x 9½ inches tall

Materials
- Medium (worsted) weight cotton yarn:
  1½ oz/75 yds/45g white
  ½ oz/25 yds/15g each peach and light peach
- Size I/9/5.5mm crochet hook
- Tapestry needle

Gauge

Gauge is not important for this project.

Pattern Notes

Chain-4 at beginning of row counts as first double crochet and chain-1 unless otherwise stated.

Chain-3 at beginning of row counts as first double crochet unless otherwise stated.

Join with slip stitch as indicated unless otherwise stated.

Special Stitches

Single crochet join (sc join): Place slip knot on hook, insert hook in indicated st, yo and draw up a lp, yo and draw through both lps on hook.

Popcorn (pc): 3 dc as indicated in instructions, drop lp from hook, insert hook from front to back in first dc of 3-dc group, pick up dropped lp, draw through st.

Dishcloth

Row 1 (RS): With white, ch 27, dc in 4th ch from hook *(sk ch count as first dc)*, dc in next ch and in each rem ch across, turn. *(25 dc)*

Row 2: Ch 4 *(see Pattern Notes)*, sk next dc, dc in next dc, [ch 1, sk next dc, dc in next dc] across, turn. *(13 dc, 12 ch-1 sps)*

Row 3: Ch 3 *(see Pattern Notes)*, [sk next ch-1 sp, dc in next dc, working in front of dc just made, dc in sk ch-1 sp] across. Fasten off white.

Row 4: With RS facing, **sc join** *(see Special Stitches)* peach in first dc, [ch 3, (dc, **pc**—*see Special Stitches*, dc) in side of last sc made, sk next 3 dc, sc in next dc] across. Fasten off peach.

Row 5: With RS facing, **join** *(see Pattern Notes)* white in first sc, ch 4, sc in 3rd ch of next ch-3, ch 1, dc in next sc, [ch 1, sc in 3rd ch of next ch-3 sp, ch 1, dc in next sc] across, turn.

Row 6: Ch 4, dc in next sc, ch 1, dc in next dc, [ch 1, dc in next sc, ch 1, dc in next dc] across, turn.

Row 7: Rep row 3. Fasten off white.

Row 8: With RS facing, sc join light peach in first dc, rep row 4. Fasten off light peach.

Rows 9–11: Rep rows 5–7.

Rows 12–15: Rep rows 4–7.

At end row 15, do not fasten off.

Edging

Rnd 1: With RS facing, sc evenly around, working 3 sc in each corner, join in first sc. Finish off and weave in ends.

Rnd 2: With RS facing, sc join peach in center sc of any corner 3-sc group, 2 sc in same sc, sc in each rem sc around, working 3 sc in center sc of each corner, join in first sc. Fasten off. ●

Sunny Day

Design by Maggie Weldon

Skill Level

 EASY

Finished Measurement

8½ inches in diameter

Materials

- Medium (worsted) weight cotton yarn:
    2 oz/100 yds/60g yellow
    1 oz/50 yds/30g orange
- Size H/8/5mm crochet hook
- Tapestry needle
- Stitch marker

Gauge

Gauge is not important for this project.

Pattern Note

Join with slip stitch as indicated unless otherwise stated.

Special Stitch

Top stitch (top st): Holding yarn at back of work, insert hook between sts, yo, pull lp through st and lp on hook.

Dishcloth

Rnd 1 (RS): With yellow, ch 4, sl st in first ch to form ring, ch 1, 15 dc in ring, **join** *(see Pattern Note)* in first dc. *(15 dc)*

Rnd 2: Ch 1, 2 dc in each dc around, join in first dc. *(30 dc)*

Rnd 3: Ch 1, [2 dc in next dc, dc in next dc] around, join in first dc. *(45 dc)*

Rnd 4: Ch 1, [2 dc in next dc, dc in each of next 8 dc] around, join in first dc. *(50 dc)*

Rnd 5: Ch 1, [2 dc in next dc, dc in each of next 4 dc] around, join in first dc. *(60 dc)*

First Ray

Row 1: With RS facing, ch 1, hdc in each of next 6 dc, place marker in next dc, turn, leaving rem dc unworked. *(6 hdc)*

Row 2: Ch 1, hdc in first hdc, [**hdc dec** *(see Stitch Guide)* in next 2 hdc] twice, hdc in last hdc, turn. *(4 sts)*

Row 3: Ch 1, [hdc dec in next 2 sts] twice, **do not turn**, working in row ends along side of Ray, sl st in each row end across, sl st in marked dc on rnd 5. *(2 sts).*

Next Ray
Make 9.

Rows 1–3: Rep rows 1–3 of First Ray. At end of last row, fasten off.

Mouth
With orange, ch 18, sl st in 2nd ch from hook and in each rem sl st across. Leaving long end for sewing, fasten off.

Using long end, sew Mouth on Dishcloth as shown in photo.

Eye
Make 2.

With orange, ch 6, sl st in 2nd ch from hook, sl st in next ch, (sl st, ch 1, sl st) in next ch, sl st in each of last 2 chs. Leaving long end for sewing, fasten off.

Using long end and tapestry needle, sew Eye on Dishcloth as shown in photo.

Face Outline
With RS of Dishcloth facing and orange, **top st** (see Special Stitch) in each st around on rnd 5. Fasten off. ●

Funfetti
Design by Carol Ballard

Skill Level
 EASY

Finished Measurements
11 inches wide x 11½ inches long

Materials
- Medium (worsted) weight cotton yarn:
  2 oz/100 yds/60g orange/green/ yellow/hot pink variegated
  ½ oz/25 yds/15g orange
- Size I/9/5.5mm crochet hook or size needed to obtain gauge
- Tapestry needle

Gauge
3 sc = 1 inch; 1 pattern row = 1 inch

Take time to check gauge.

Pattern Notes
Chain-3 at beginning of row counts as first double crochet unless otherwise stated.

Join with slip stitch as indicated unless otherwise stated.

Special Stitches
Shell: 7 dc as indicated in instructions.

Single crochet join (sc join): Place slip knot on hook, insert hook in indicated st, yo and draw up a lp, yo and draw through both lps on hook.

Dishcloth

Row 1 (RS): With variegated, ch 31, sc in 2nd ch from hook and in each rem ch across, turn. *(30 sc)*

Row 2: Ch 3 *(see Pattern Notes)*, dc in next sc, [sk next 2 sc, **shell** *(see Special Stitches)* in next sc, sk next 2 sc, dc in each of next 2 sc] across, turn. *(4 shells, 10 dc)*

Row 3: Ch 3, dc in next dc, [sk next 3 dc, shell in next dc, sk next 3 dc, dc in each of next 2 dc] across, turn.

Rows 4–13: [Rep row 3] 10 times.

Row 14: Ch 1, sc in first dc, sc in next dc, [ch 2, sk next 3 dc, sc in next dc, ch 2, sk next 3 dc, sc in each of next 2 dc] across, turn.

Row 15: Ch 1, sc in first sc, sc in next sc, [2 sc in next ch-2 sp, sc in next sc, 2 sc in next ch-2 sp, sc in each of next 2 sc] across. Fasten off. *(30 sc)*

Edging

Rnd 1: With RS facing, **sc join** *(see Special Stitches)* orange in first sc on last row, 2 sc in same st, sc in each of next 28 sc, 3 sc in last sc, working in row ends along side, sc in next row end, 2 sc in each of next 12 row ends, sc in last row end, working across opposite side of foundation ch, 3 sc in first ch, sc in each of next 28 chs, 3 sc in last ch; working in row ends along opposite side, sc in next row end, 2 sc in each of next 12 row ends, sc in last row end, **join** *(see Pattern Notes)* in first sc. Fasten off. ●

Tropical Breeze

Design by Maggie Weldon

Skill Level

 EASY

Finished Measurements

7½ inches wide x 9 inches long

Materials

- Medium (worsted) weight cotton yarn:
  1½ oz/75 yds/45g orange
  1 oz/50 yds/30g each dark pink and orange/green/yellow/hot pink variegated
- Size H/8/5mm crochet hook
- Tapestry needle

4 MEDIUM

Gauge

Gauge is not important for this project.

Pattern Notes

Chain-3 at beginning of row counts as first double crochet unless otherwise stated.

Join with slip stitch as indicated unless otherwise stated.

Special Stitch

Long front post double crochet (long fpdc): Yo, insert hook from front to back to front around post of indicated st, yo, pull up lp to height of sts on hook, [yo and draw through 2 lps on hook] twice.

Dishcloth

Row 1 (RS): With orange, ch 28, dc in 4th ch from hook *(sk chs count as first dc)*, dc in next ch and in each rem ch across, turn. *(26 dc)*

Row 2: Ch 1, sc in each dc across, **changing color** *(see Stitch Guide)* to variegated in last st, turn. Fasten off orange.

Row 3: With variegated, **ch 3** *(see Pattern Notes)*, dc in next sc, **long fpdc** *(see Special Stitch)* around next dc 2 rows below, *dc in each of next 2 sts**, long fpdc around next dc 2 rows below, rep from * across, ending last rep at **, turn.

Row 4: Ch 1, sc in each dc across, changing color to dark pink in last st, turn. Fasten off variegated.

Row 5: With pink, ch 3, dc in next sc, [long fpdc around next long fpdc 2 rows below, dc in each of next 2 sc] across, turn.

Row 6: Ch 1, sc in each dc across, changing color to variegated in last st, turn. Fasten off pink.

Row 7: With variegated, ch 3, dc in next sc, [long fpdc around next long fpdc 2 rows below, dc in each of next 2 sc] across, turn.

Row 8: Ch 1, sc in each dc across, changing color to orange in last st, turn. Fasten off variegated.

Row 9: With orange, ch 3, dc in next sc, [long fpdc around next long fpdc 2 rows below, dc in each of next 2 sc] across, turn.

Row 10: Ch 1, sc in each dc across, changing color to variegated in last st, turn. Fasten off orange.

Row 11: Rep row 7.

Rows 12–19: Rep rows 4–11.

Rows 20–24: Rep rows 4–8.

At end of row 24, fasten off variegated.

Edging

Rnd 1: With RS facing, **join** *(see Pattern Notes)* orange in first sc on last row, ch 3, 4 dc in same sc *(corner made)*, dc evenly around, working 5 dc in each corner, join in top of beg ch-3. Fasten off. ●

Orange Slice

Design by Maggie Weldon

Skill Level

 EASY

Finished Measurement

8 inches in diameter

Materials
- Medium (worsted) weight cotton yarn:
   1½ oz/75 yds/45g orange
   ½ oz/25 yds/15g white
- Size H/8/5mm crochet hook
- Tapestry needle

4
MEDIUM

Gauge

Gauge is not important for this project.

Pattern Notes

Join with slip stitch as indicated unless otherwise stated.

Chain-3 at beginning of round counts as first double crochet unless otherwise stated.

Special Stitches

Single crochet join (sc join): Place slip knot on hook, insert hook in indicated st, yo and draw up a lp, yo and draw through both lps on hook.

Spike: Yo 7 times, insert hook from front to back to front around post of indicated st, yo, pull up lp, [yo and draw through 2 lps on hook] 8 times.

Dishcloth

Rnd 1 (RS): With white, ch 2, 8 sc in 2nd ch from hook, **join** *(see Pattern Notes)* in **back lp** *(see Stitch Guide)* of first sc. Fasten off. *(8 sc)*

Rnd 2: With RS facing, **sc join** *(see Special Stitches)* orange in back lp of any sc, working in back lp, 2 sc in next sc, [sc in next sc, 2 sc in next sc] around, join in back lp of first sc. *(12 sc)*

Rnd 3: Ch 3 *(see Pattern Notes)*, working in back lps, dc in same st as joining, 2 dc in each rem dc around, join in back lp of 3rd ch of beg ch-3. *(24 dc)*

Rnd 4: Ch 3, working in back lps, dc in same st as joining, dc in next dc, [2 dc in next dc, dc in next dc] around, join in back lp of 3rd ch of beg ch-3. *(36 dc)*

Rnd 5: Ch 3, working in back lps, dc in same st as joining, dc in each of next 2 dc, [2 dc in next dc, dc in each of next 2 dc] around, join in back lp of 3rd ch of beg ch-3. *(48 dc)*

Rnd 6: Ch 3, working in back lps, dc in same st as joining, dc in each of next 2 dc, [2 dc in next dc, dc in each of next 2 dc] around, join in top of beg ch-3. Fasten off. *(64 dc)*

Rnd 7: With RS facing, sc join white in any dc, sc in each of next 7 dc, [**spike** *(see Special Stitches)* around next sc on rnd 1, sc in each of next 8 dc] around, spike in last sc on rnd 1, join in first sc. Fasten off. *(64 sc, 8 spikes)*

Rnd 8: With RS facing, join orange in any sc, ch 1, hdc in same st as joining, hdc in each rem st around, join in first hdc. *(72 hdc)*

Rnd 9: Ch 1, sc in each hdc around, join in first sc. Fasten off. *(72 sc)* ●

Popcorn

Design by Kathleen Stuart

Skill Level

■■□□ EASY

Finished Measurements

8 inches wide x 10 inches long

Materials

- Medium (worsted) weight cotton yarn:
  1½ oz/75 yds/45g white
  ½ oz/25 yds/15g red
  ¼ oz/13 yds/8g yellow
- Size J/10/6mm crochet hook
- Tapestry needle

Gauge

Gauge is not important for this project.

Pattern Notes

Tub is worked in back loops only unless otherwise stated.

Do not fasten off yarn; carry unused color along edge until next needed.

Special Stitches

Single crochet join (sc join): Place slip knot on hook, insert hook in indicated st, yo and draw up a lp, yo and draw through both lps on hook.

Popcorn (pc): 3 dc as indicated in instructions, drop lp from hook, insert hook from front to back in first dc of 3-dc group, pick up dropped lp, draw through st.

Dishcloth

Tub

Row 1 (RS): With red, ch 26, working in **back lps** (see Stitch Guide and Pattern Notes), sc in 2nd ch from hook and in each rem ch across, turn. *(25 sc)*

Row 2: Ch 1, sc in each sc across, **changing color** (see Stitch Guide) to white in last sc, turn. **Do not fasten off red** (see Pattern Notes).

Row 3: With white, ch 1, sc in each sc across, turn.

Row 4: Rep row 3, changing color to red in last sc, turn.

Row 5: With red, ch 1, sc in each sc across, turn.

Rows 6–25: [Rep rows 2–5 consecutively] 5 times.

Row 26: Ch 1, sc in each sc across, turn.

Row 27: Ch 1, sl st in each sc across. Fasten off. *(25 sl sts)*

Popcorn

Row 1: With RS facing, working in row ends along side of Tub, **sc join** *(see Special Stitches)* white in first row end, sc in each rem row end across, turn. *(27 sc)*

Row 2: Ch 1, sc in each sc across, turn.

Row 3: Ch 1, sl st in first sc, [**pc** *(see Special Stitches)* in next sc, sc in next sc] across, turn. *(13 pc)*

Row 4: Ch 1, sl st in first sc, sc in next pc, [sc in next sc, sc in next pc] across, turn. *(25 sc)*

Rows 5–12: [Rep rows 3 and 4 alternately] 4 times. *(17 sc at end of row 12)*

At end row 12, fasten off.

Letter P
Make 2.

With yellow, ch 15, sl st in 11th ch from hook. Leaving long end for sewing, fasten off.

Letter O
Make 2.

With yellow, ch 15, sl st in first ch to form ring. Leaving long end for sewing, fasten off.

Letter C

With yellow, ch 15. Leaving long end for sewing, fasten off.

Letter R

With yellow, ch 15, sl st in 11th ch from hook, ch 5. Leaving long end for sewing, fasten off.

Letter N

With yellow, ch 21. Leaving long end for sewing, fasten off.

Finishing

Using long ends and tapestry needle, sew Letters on Tub as shown in photo. ●

Retro Ripple

Design by Carol Ballard

Skill Level
 EASY

Finished Measurements
9 inches wide x 10½ inches long

Materials
- Size 10 crochet cotton:
    125 yds each white and black
    30 yds red
- Size E/4/3.5mm crochet hook or size needed to obtain gauge
- Tapestry needle

Gauge

With 2 strands held tog: 5 dc = 1 inch; 2 dc rows = 1 inch

Take time to check gauge.

Pattern Notes

Hold 2 strands together unless otherwise stated.

Chain-3 at beginning of row counts as first double crochet unless otherwise stated.

Join with slip stitch as indicated unless otherwise stated.

Special Stitch

Single crochet join (sc join): Place slip knot on hook, insert hook in indicated st, yo and draw up a lp, yo and draw through both lps on hook.

Dishcloth

Row 1 (RS): With **2 strands white held tog** *(see Pattern Notes)*, ch 46, sc in 2nd ch from hook and in each rem ch across, turn. *(45 sc)*

Row 2: Ch 3 *(see Pattern Notes)*, dc in each of next 6 sc, (dc, ch 2, dc) in next sc, [dc in each of next 6 sc, sk next 2 sc, dc in each of next 6 sc, (dc, ch 2, dc) in next sc] twice, dc in each of next 7 sc, turn.

Row 3: Ch 3, **dc dec** *(see Stitch Guide)* in next 2 sts, dc in each of next 5 dc, (dc, ch 2, dc) in next ch-2 sp, [dc in each of next 6 dc, sk next 2 dc, dc in each of next 6 dc, (dc, ch 2, dc) in next ch-2 sp] twice, dc in each of next 5 dc, dc dec in next 2 dc, dc in last dc, **changing color** *(see Stitch Guide)* to black in last st, turn.

Row 4: With black, ch 3, dc dec in next 2 sts, dc in each of next 5 dc, (dc, ch 2, dc) in next ch-2 sp, [dc in each of next 6 dc, sk next 2 dc, dc in each of next 6 dc, (dc, ch 2, dc) in next ch-2 sp] twice, dc in each of next 5 dc, dc dec in next 2 sts, dc in last dc, turn.

Row 5: Rep row 4, changing color to white in last st, turn.

Row 6: With white, rep row 4.

Row 7: Rep row 4, changing color to black in last st, turn.

Rows 8–19: [Rep rows 4–7 consecutively] 3 times.

Rows 20 & 21: Rep rows 4 and 5. At end of row 21, fasten off.

Edging

Rnd 1: With RS facing, **sc join** *(see Special Stitch)* red in first dc of last row, **sc dec** *(see Stitch Guide)* in next 2 sts, sc in each of next 5 dc, 4 sc in next ch-2 sp, [sc in each of next 6 dc, sk next 2 dc, sc in each of next 6 dc, 4 sc in next ch-2 sp] twice, sc in each of next 5 dc, sc dec in next 2 sts, 2 sc in last dc, working in row ends along side of piece, 2 sc in each row end across, working across opposite side of foundation ch, 2 sc in first ch, sk next ch, [sc in each of next 6 chs, sk next ch sc in each of next 6 chs, 4 sc in next ch] twice, sk next ch, sc in each of next 6 chs, sk next ch, sc in each of next 6 chs, 2 sc in last ch, working in row ends along opposite side, 2 sc in each row end across, **join** *(see Pattern Notes)* in first sc.

Rnd 2: Ch 1, sc in each sc around, join in first sc. Fasten off. ●

Flag

Design by Maggie Weldon

Skill Level

 EASY

Finished Measurements

9 inches wide x 8 inches long

Materials

- Medium (worsted) weight cotton yarn:
  1 oz/50 yds/30g each blue, white and red
  ½ oz/25 yds/15g gold
- Size H/8/5mm crochet hook
- Tapestry needle

Gauge

Gauge is not important for this project.

Pattern Notes

When changing color, drop old color and complete stitch with new color. Leave old color until next needed.

Join with slip stitch as indicated unless otherwise stated.

Chain-3 at beginning of round counts as first double crochet unless otherwise stated.

Special Stitch

Single crochet join (sc join): Place slip knot on hook, insert hook in indicated st, yo and draw up a lp, yo and draw through both lps on hook.

Dishcloth

Row 1 (WS): With blue, ch 8, **change color** (see Stitch Guide and Pattern Notes) to red in next ch, with red, ch 17, sc in 2nd ch from hook, sc in each of next 15

chs, change color to blue, with blue, sc in next 9 chs, turn. (24 sc)

Row 2 (RS): Ch 1, sc in each of first 9 sc, change color to red, sc in each of next 15 sc, change color to white in last st, turn.

Row 3: With white, ch 1, sc in each of first 15 sc, change color to blue, with blue, sc in each of next 9 sc, turn.

Row 4: Ch 1, sc in each of first 9 sc, change color to white, with white, sc in next 15 sc, change color to red in last st, turn.

Row 5: With red, ch 1, sc in each of first 15 sc, change color to blue, with blue, sc in each of next 9 sc, turn.

Row 6: Ch 1, sc in each of first 9 sc, change color to red, with red, sc in each of next 15 sc, change color to white in last st, turn.

Rows 7–14: [Rep rows 3–6 consecutively] twice.

At end of row 14, fasten off blue.

Row 15: With white, ch 1, sc in each sc across, turn.

Row 16: Rep row 15, change color to red in last st.

Rows 17 & 18: With red, rep rows 15 and 16, change color to white in last st of row 18.

Rows 19–26: [Rep rows 15–18 consecutively] twice.

At end of row 26, fasten off.

Edging

Rnd 1: With RS facing, **sc join** (see Special Stitch) blue in last sc on row 26, 2 sc in same sc, working in row ends along side, sc evenly across side, working across opposite side of foundation ch, 3 sc in first ch, sc in each of next 22 chs, 3 sc in last ch, working in row ends along opposite side, sc evenly along side, working across row 26, 3 sc in first sc, sc in each of next 22 sc, **join** (see Pattern Notes) in first sc. Fasten off.

Rnd 2: With RS facing, join gold in center sc of any corner 3-sc group, **ch 3** (see Pattern Notes), (dc, ch 2, 2 dc) in same sp, dc in each rem sc around, working (2 dc, ch 2, 2 dc) in each corner ch-2 sp, join in top of beg ch-3. Fasten off.

Finishing

Using white and tapestry needle, embroider cross stitches for stars as shown in photo. ●

Sunflower in Circle

Design by Maggie Weldon

Skill Level
 EASY

Finished Measurement
9½ inches in diameter

Materials
- Medium (worsted) weight cotton yarn:
    1 oz/50 yds/30g dark green
    ½ oz/25 yds/15g gold
    ¼ oz/13 yds/8g brown
- Size H/8/5mm crochet hook
- Tapestry needle

4
MEDIUM

Gauge
Gauge is not important for this project.

Pattern Notes
Join with slip stitch as indicated unless otherwise stated.

Chain-3 at beginning of round counts as first double crochet unless otherwise stated.

Special Stitch

Single crochet join (sc join): Place slip knot on hook, insert hook in indicated st, yo and draw up a lp, yo and draw through both lps on hook.

Dishcloth

Rnd 1 (RS): With brown, ch 2, 6 sc in 2nd ch from hook, **join** *(see Pattern Notes)* in first sc. *(6 sc)*

Rnd 2: Ch 1, [sc, ch 1] twice in each sc around, join in first sc. *(12 sc, 12 ch-1 sps)*

Rnds 3 & 4: Sl st in first ch-1 sp, ch 1, sc in same sp, ch 1, [sc in next ch-1 sp, ch 1] around, join in first sc. Fasten off brown.

Rnd 5: With RS facing, **sc join** *(see Special Stitch)* gold in any ch-1 sp, (dc, tr, ch 2, sl st in last tr made, tr, dc, sc, sl st) in same ch-1 sp, (sc, dc, tr, ch 2, sl st in last tr made, tr, dc, sc, sl st) in each rem ch-1 sp around, join in first sc. *(12 petals)*

Rnd 6: Working behind petals, [ch 4, sl st in sp between next 2 petals] around. Fasten off gold. *(12 ch-4 lps)*

Rnd 7: With RS facing, join green in any ch-4 lp, **ch 3** *(see Pattern Notes)*, 3 dc in same lp, 4 dc in each rem ch-4 lp around, join in top of beg ch-3. *(48 dc)*

Rnd 8: Ch 3, dc in same st as joining, dc in each of next 3 dc, [2 dc in next dc, dc in each of next 3 dc] around, join in top of beg ch-3. Fasten off green. *(60 dc)*

Rnd 9: With RS facing, sc join gold in any dc, ch 2, sk next dc, [sc in next dc, ch 2, sk next dc] around, join in first sc. Fasten off gold. *(30 sc, 30 ch-2 sps)*

Rnd 10: With RS facing, join green in any ch-2 sp, ch 3, 2 dc in same sp, [3 dc in next ch-2 sp] 3 times, 2 dc in next ch-2 sp, *[3 dc in next ch-2 sp] 4 times, 2 dc in next ch-2 sp, rep from * 4 times, join in top of beg ch-3. *(84 dc)*

Rnd 11: Ch 3, dc in same st as joining, dc in each of next 6 dc, [2 dc in next dc, dc in each of next 6 dc] around, join in top of beg ch-3. Fasten off green. *(96 dc)*

Rnd 12: With gold, rep rnd 9. *(48 sc, 48 ch-2 sps)*

Fasten off. ●

Sunflower

Design by Carol Ballard

Skill Level
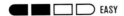 EASY

Finished Measurement
9 inches in diameter

Materials
- Medium (worsted) weight cotton yarn:
    2 oz/100 yds/60g yellow
    ½ oz/25 yds/15g black
- Size I/9/5.5mm crochet hook or size needed to obtain gauge
- Tapestry needle

Gauge

6 dc = 2 inches; 3 rows dc = 2 inches

Take time to check gauge.

Pattern Notes

Join with slip stitch as indicated unless otherwise stated.

Chain-3 at beginning of round counts as first double crochet unless otherwise stated.

Special Stitch

Single crochet join (sc join): Place slip knot on hook, insert hook in indicated st, yo and draw up a lp, yo and draw through both lps on hook.

Dishcloth

Rnd 1 (RS): With black, ch 2, 6 sc in 2nd ch from hook, **join** *(see Pattern Notes)* in first sc. *(6 sc)*

Rnd 2: Ch 1, 2 sc in each sc around, join in **front lp** *(see Stitch Guide)* of first sc. *(12 sc)*

Rnd 3: Ch 1, working in front lps, sc in first sc, ch 3, [sc in next sc, ch 3] 11 times, join in back lp of first sc on rnd 2. *(12 sc, 12 ch-3 lps)*

Rnd 4: Ch 1, working in **back lps** *(see Stitch Guide)* on rnd 2 and behind ch-3 lps, 2 sc in first sc, sc in next sc, [2 sc in next sc, sc in next sc] 5 times, join in first sc. *(18 sc)*

Rnd 5: Ch 1, 2 sc in first sc, sc in each of next 2 sc, [2 sc in next sc, sc in each of next 2 sc] 5 times, join in front lp of first sc. *(24 sc)*

Rnd 6: Ch 1, working in front lps, sc in first sc, ch 3, [sc in next sc, ch 3] 23 times, join in back lp of first sc on rnd 4. *(24 sc, 24 ch-3 lps)*

Rnd 7: Ch 1, working in back lps on rnd 5 and behind ch-3 lps, sc in each sc around, join in first sc. *(24 sc)*

Rnd 8: Ch 1, 2 sc in first sc, sc in each of next 3 sc, [2 sc in next sc, sc in each of next 3 sc] 5 times, join in first sc. Fasten off black. *(30 sc)*

Rnd 9: With RS facing, join yellow in any sc, **ch 3** *(see Pattern Notes)*, dc in first sc, dc in each of next 4 sc, [2 dc in next sc, dc in each of next 3 sc, 2 dc in next sc] 4 times, dc in each rem sc around, join in top of beg ch-3. *(39 dc)*

Rnd 10: Ch 3, dc in first dc, dc in next dc, **fpdc** *(see Stitch Guide)* around next dc, [2 dc in next dc, dc in next dc, fpdc around next dc] 12 times, join in top of beg ch-3. *(39 dc, 13 fpdc)*

Rnd 11: Ch 3, dc in first dc, dc in each of next 2 dc, fpdc around next fpdc, [2 dc in next dc, dc in each of next 2 dc, fpdc around next fpdc] 12 times, join in top of beg ch-3. *(52 dc, 13 fpdc)*

Rnd 12: Ch 3, dc in first dc, dc in each of next 3 dc, fpdc around next fpdc, [2 dc in next dc, dc in each of next 3 dc, fpdc around next fpdc] 12 times, join in top of beg ch-3. *(65 dc, 13 fpdc)*

Rnd 13: Ch 1, hdc in first dc, hdc in next dc, 3 dc in next dc, hdc in each of next 2 dc, **fpsc** *(see Stitch Guide)* around next fpdc, [hdc in each of next 2 dc, 3 dc in next dc, hdc in each of next 2 dc, fpsc around next fpdc] 12 times, join in first hdc. Fasten off. ●

Golden Fans

Design by Renae Hopkins

Skill Level

 EASY

Finished Measurements

10½ inches wide x 9½ inches long

Materials

- Medium (worsted) weight cotton yarn:
  2 oz/100 yds/60g yellow
- Size H/8/5mm crochet hook
- Tapestry needle

4 MEDIUM

Gauge

Gauge is not important for this project.

Pattern Note

Join with slip stitch as indicated unless otherwise stated.

Special Stitch

Fan: (2 dc, ch 1, 2 dc) as indicated in instructions.

Dishcloth

Row 1 (RS): Ch 38, sc in 2nd ch from hook, [sk next 2 chs, **fan** (see Special Stitch) in next ch, sk next 2 chs, sc in next ch] across, turn. (7 sc, 6 fans)

Row 2: Ch 1, 3 dc in first sc, [sc in ch-1 sp of next fan, fan in next sc] 5 times, sc in ch-1 sp of next fan, 3 dc in last sc, turn. (6 dc, 6 sc, 5 fans)

Row 3: Ch 1, sc in first dc, sk next 2 dc, [fan in next sc, sc in ch-1 sp of next fan] 5 times, fan in next sc, sk next 2 dc, sc in last dc, turn. (7 sc, 6 fans)

Rows 4–19: [Rep rows 2 and 3 alternately] 8 times.

At end of row 19, do not turn.

Edging

Rnd 1: Ch 1, sc evenly around entire piece, working 3 sc in each corner, **join** (see Pattern Note) in first sc. Fasten off. ●

Ruffled Square

Design by Maggie Weldon

Skill Level

 EASY

Finished Measurement

9½ inches square

Materials

- Medium (worsted) weight cotton yarn: 1 oz/50 yds/30g each white and pink
- Size H/8/5mm crochet hook
- Tapestry needle

Gauge

Gauge is not important for this project.

Pattern Notes

Chain-3 at beginning of round counts as first double crochet unless otherwise stated.

Chain-1, single crochet at end of round counts as last chain-2 space unless otherwise stated.

Join with slip stitch as indicated unless otherwise stated.

Chain-5 at beginning of round counts as first double crochet and chain-2 space unless otherwise stated.

Chain-6 at beginning of round counts as first double crochet and chain-3 space unless otherwise stated.

Chain-1, half double crochet at end of round counts as last chain-3 space unless otherwise stated.

Chain-2, half double crochet at end of round counts as last chain-4 space unless otherwise stated.

Special Stitch

Single crochet join (sc join): Place slip knot on hook, insert hook in indicated st, yo and draw up a lp, yo and draw through both lps on hook.

Dishcloth

Rnd 1 (RS): With white, ch 5, sl st in first ch to form ring, **ch 3** *(see Pattern Notes)*, 2 dc in ring, [ch 2, 3 dc in ring] 3 times, **(ch 1, sc)** *(see Pattern Notes)* in first dc. *(12 dc, 4 ch-2 sps)*

Rnd 2: Ch 1, 2 sc in first ch-2 sp, sc in each of next 3 dc, [(2 sc, ch 2, 2 sc) in next ch-2 sp, sc in each of next 3 dc] 3 times, 2 sc in first ch-2 sp, (ch 1, sc) in **back lp** *(see Stitch Guide)* of first sc. Fasten off white. *(28 sc, 4 ch-2 sps)*

Rnd 3: With RS facing, **sc join** *(see Special Stitch)* pink in any ch-2 sp, (sc, ch 2, 2 sc) in same sp, working in **back lps** *(see Stitch Guide)*, sc in each sc across to next corner ch-2 sp, *(2 sc, ch 2, 2 sc) in corner ch-2 sp, sc in each sc across to next corner ch-2 sp, rep from * around, **join** (see Pattern Notes) in first sc. Fasten off pink. (44 sc, 4 ch-2 sps)

Rnd 4: With RS facing, join white in any ch-2 sp, **ch 5** (see Pattern Notes), dc in same sp, working in back lps, dc in each rem sc across to next corner, *(dc, ch 2, dc) in corner ch-2 sp, dc in next sc and in each rem sc across to next corner ch-2 sp, rep from * around, join in 3rd ch of beg ch-5. (52 dc, 4 ch-2 sps)

Rnd 5: Sl st in next ch-2 sp, ch 5, dc in same sp, working in back lps, dc in next dc and in each rem dc across to next corner, *(dc, ch 2, dc) in corner ch-2 sp, dc in next dc and in each rem dc across to next corner ch-2 sp, rep from * around, join in 3rd ch of beg ch-5. (60 dc, 4 ch-2 sps)

Rnd 6: Sl st in next ch-2 sp, **ch 6** (see Pattern Notes), dc in same sp, working in back lps, dc in next dc and in each rem dc across to next corner, *(dc, ch 3, dc) in corner ch-2 sp, dc in next dc and in each rem dc

across to next corner ch-2 sp, rep from * around, join in 3rd ch of beg ch-6. Fasten off. (68 dc, 4 ch-3 sps)

Rnd 7: With RS facing, sc join pink in any corner ch-3 sp, 2 sc in same sp, working in back lps, sc in next dc and in each rem dc across to next corner ch-3 sp, *3 sc in next ch-3 sp, sc in next dc and in each rem dc across to next corner ch-3 sp, rep from * around, join in first sc. (80 sc)

Rnd 8: Ch 1, sc in first st, ch 3, [sc in next sc, ch 3] twice, *[sk next sc, sc in next sc, ch 3] across to last sc before next corner 3-sc group, sk last sc, [sc in next sc, ch 3] 3 times, rep from * twice, sk next sc, sc in next sc, [ch 3, sk next sc, sc in next sc] across to last sc, sk last sc, **(ch 1, hdc)** (see Pattern Notes) in first sc. (44 ch-3 sps)

Rnd 9: Ch 1, sc in first ch-3 sp, [ch 4, sc in next ch-3 sp] around, **(ch 2, hdc)** (see Pattern Notes) in first sc.

Rnd 10: Ch 1, sc in first ch-4 sp, ch 5, [sc in next ch-4 sp, ch 5] around, join in first sc. Fasten off. ●

Candy Corn

Design by Maggie Weldon

Skill Level
 ◼◼◻◻◻ EASY

Finished Measurements
8½ inches wide at bottom x 8½ inches long

Materials
- Medium (worsted) weight cotton yarn:
  1 oz/50 yds/30g each orange and yellow
  ½ oz/25 yds/15g white
- Size H/8/5mm crochet hook
- Tapestry needle

4 MEDIUM

Gauge
Gauge is not important for this project.

Pattern Notes
Chain-2 at beginning of row counts as first half double crochet unless otherwise stated.

Work in back loops unless otherwise stated.

Dishcloth
Row 1 (RS): Beg at top with white, **ch 2** (see Pattern Notes), 3 sc in 2nd ch from hook, turn. (3 sc)

Row 2: Ch 2, working in **back lps** (see Stitch Guide and Pattern Notes), sc in first sc, 2 sc in next sc, (sc, hdc) in last sc, turn. (2 hdc, 4 sc)

Row 3: Ch 2, 2 sc in next sc, sc in each of next 2 sc, 2 sc in next sc, hdc in last hdc, turn. *(2 hdc, 6 sc)*

Row 4: Ch 2, sc in next sc, 2 sc in next sc, sc in each of next 2 sc, 2 sc in next sc, sc in next sc, hdc in last hdc, turn. *(2 hdc, 8 sc)*

Row 5: Ch 2, sc in each of next 2 sc, 2 sc in next sc, sc in each of next 2 sc, 2 sc in next sc, sc in each of next 2 sc, hdc in last hdc, turn. *(2 hdc, 10 sc)*

Row 6: Ch 2, sc in each of next 3 sc, 2 sc in next sc, sc in each of next 2 sc, 2 sc in next sc, sc in each of next 3 sc, hdc in last hdc, turn. *(2 hdc, 12 sc)*

Row 7: Ch 2, sc in each of next 4 sc, 2 sc in next sc, sc in each of next 2 sc, 2 sc in next sc, sc in each of next 4 sc, hdc in last hdc, turn. *(2 hdc, 14 sc)*

Row 8: Ch 2, sc in each of next 5 sc, 2 sc in next sc, sc in each of next 2 sc, 2 sc in next sc, sc in each of next 5 sc, hdc in last hdc, **changing color** *(see Stitch Guide)* to orange in last st, turn. Fasten off white. *(2 hdc, 16 sc)*

Row 9: Ch 2, sc in next sc and in each rem sc across to last hdc, hdc in last hdc, turn. *(2 hdc, 16 sc)*

Row 10: Ch 2, sc in each of next 4 sc, 2 sc in next sc, sc in each of next 6 sc, 2 sc in next sc, sc in each of next 4 sc, hdc in last hdc, turn. *(2 hdc, 18 sc)*

Row 11: Rep row 9.

Row 12: Ch 2, sc in each of next 5 sc, 2 sc in next sc, sc in each of next 6 sc, 2 sc in next sc, sc in each of next 5 sc, hdc in last hdc, turn. *(2 hdc, 20 sc)*

Row 13: Rep row 9.

Row 14: Ch 2, sc in each of next 6 sc, 2 sc in next sc, sc in each of next 6 sc, 2 sc in next sc, sc in each of next 6 sc, hdc in last hdc, turn. *(2 hdc, 22 sc)*

Row 15: Rep row 9.

Row 16: Ch 2, sc in each of next 7 sc, 2 sc in next sc, sc in each of next 6 sc, 2 sc in next sc, sc in each of next 7 sc, hdc in last hdc, turn. *(2 hdc, 24 sc)*

Row 17: Rep row 9.

Row 18: Ch 2, sc in each of next 8 sc, 2 sc in next sc, sc in each of next 6 sc, 2 sc in next sc, sc in each of next 8 sc, hdc in last hdc, turn. *(2 hdc, 26 sc)*

Row 19: Rep row 9.

Row 20: Ch 2, sc in each of next 9 sc, 2 sc in next sc, sc in each of next 6 sc, 2 sc in next sc, sc in each of next 9 sc, hdc in last hdc, turn. *(2 hdc, 28 sc)*

Row 21: Rep row 9.

Row 22: Ch 2, sc in each of next 10 sc, 2 sc in next sc, sc in each of next 6 sc, 2 sc in next sc, sc in each of next 10 sc, hdc in last hdc, changing color to yellow in last st, turn. Fasten off orange. *(2 hdc, 30 sc)*

Row 23: Rep row 9.

Row 24: Ch 2, sc in each of next 9 sc, 2 sc in next sc, sc in each of next 10 sc, 2 sc in next sc, sc in each of next 9 sc, hdc in last hdc, turn. *(2 hdc, 32 sc)*

Row 25: Rep row 9.

Row 26: Ch 2, sc in each of next 10 sc, 2 sc in next sc, sc in each of next 10 sc, 2 sc in next sc, sc in each of next 10 sc, hdc in last hdc, turn. *(2 hdc, 34 sc)*

Rows 27 & 28: [Rep row 9] twice.

Row 29: Ch 1, sc in next sc and in each rem sc across to last hdc, sl st in last hdc. Fasten off and weave in ends. ●

Thanksgiving Turkey

Design by Maggie Weldon

Skill Level

 EASY

Finished Measurements

11 inches wide x 8 inches long

Materials

- Medium (worsted) weight cotton yarn:
  1 oz/50 yds/30g each multicolored and beige
  ½ oz/25 yds/15g each pink, maroon and brown
- Size H/8/5mm crochet hook
- Tapestry needle
- Stitch marker

4 MEDIUM

Gauge

Gauge is not important for this project.

Pattern Notes

Join with slip stitch as indicated unless otherwise stated.

Chain-3 at beginning of row counts as first double crochet unless otherwise stated.

Chain-2 at beginning of row or round counts as first half double crochet unless otherwise stated.

Special Stitch

Shell: 9 dc in st or sp as indicated in instructions.

Dishcloth

Tail

Row 1 (WS): With multicolored, ch 14, dc in 4th ch from hook and in each of next 2 chs, hdc in each of next 4 chs, sc in each of next 4 chs, turn. *(12 sts)*

Row 2 (RS): Ch 1, working in **back lps** *(see Stitch Guide)*, sc in each of next 4 sc, hdc in each of next 4 hdc, dc in each of next 3 dc, **shell** *(see Special Stitch)* around beg ch-3 on row 1, place marker in first dc on shell, sl st in last foundation ch. Fasten off. *(4 sc, 4 hdc, 12 dc)*

Row 3: With WS facing and working in **front lps** *(see Stitch Guide)*, **join** *(see Pattern Notes)* in marked st, **ch 3** *(see Pattern Notes)*, dc in each of next 3 dc, hdc in each of next 4 hdc, sc in each of next 4 sc, turn.

Row 4: Ch 1, working in back lps, sc in each of first 4 sc, hdc in each of next 4 hdc, dc in each of next 3 dc, shell around beg ch-3 on previous row, sl st in marked st, move marker to first dc of shell. Fasten off.

Rows 5–26: [Rep rows 3 and 4 alternately] 11 times.

Head

Rnd 1 (RS): With beige, ch 4, sl st in first ch to form ring, **ch 2** (see Pattern Notes), 9 hdc in ring, join in top of beg ch-2. (10 hdc)

Rnd 2: Ch 3, dc in first st, 2 dc in each rem sts around, join in top of beg ch-3, do not fasten off. (20 dc)

Body

Row 1: Now working in rows, ch 2, 2 hdc in first st, hdc in each of next 3 sts, 3 hdc in next st, turn, leaving rem sts unworked. (9 hdc)

Row 2: Ch 2, hdc in first st and in each rem st across to last st, 2 hdc in last st, turn. (11 hdc)

Rows 3–6: Ch 2, hdc in next st and in each rem st across, turn.

Rows 7 & 8: Ch 1, **hdc dec** (see Stitch Guide) in first 2 sts, hdc in each rem st across to last 2 sts, hdc dec in last 2 sts, turn. Do not fasten off. (7 sts)

Feet

Row 1: Sl st in each of first 2 sts, ch 1, [(sc, hdc, 2 dc) in next st, (2 dc, hdc, sc) in next st, sl st in next st] twice. Fasten off.

Beak

With pink, ch 4, 3 dc in 4th ch from hook. Leaving long end for sewing, fasten off.

Wattle

With maroon, ch 12, sc in 2nd ch from hook and in each of next 6 chs, sl st in each of next 4 chs. Leaving long end for sewing, fasten off.

Finishing

With long ends sew Beak and Wattle on Head as shown in photo. With brown, using **French knot** (see illustration), embroider eyes on Head as shown in photo.

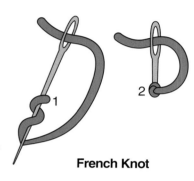

French Knot

Sew Tail to each side of Body and to top of Head. ●

Pumpkin

Design by Maggie Weldon

Skill Level

 EASY

Finished Measurement

8¼ inches in diameter

Materials
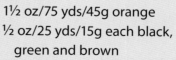

- Medium (worsted) weight cotton yarn:
    1½ oz/75 yds/45g orange
    ½ oz/25 yds/15g each black, green and brown
- Size H/8/5mm crochet hook
- Tapestry needle

Gauge

Gauge is not important for this project.

Pattern Notes

Chain-3 at beginning of round counts as first double crochet unless otherwise stated.

Join with slip stitch as indicated unless otherwise stated.

Dishcloth

Pumpkin

Rnd 1 (RS): With orange, ch 4, sl st in first ch to form ring, **ch 3** *(see Pattern Notes)*, 11 dc in ring, **join** *(see Pattern Notes)* in top of beg ch-3. *(12 dc)*

Rnd 2: Ch 3, dc in first dc, 2 dc in each rem dc around, join in top of beg ch-3. *(24 dc)*

Rnd 3: Ch 3, dc in first dc, dc in next dc, [2 dc in next dc, dc in next dc] 11 times, join in top of beg ch-3. *(36 dc)*

Rnd 4: Ch 3, dc in first dc, dc in each of next 2 dc, [2 dc in next dc, dc in each of next 2 dc] 11 times, join in top of beg ch-3. *(48 dc)*

Rnd 5: Ch 3, dc in first dc, dc in each of next 3 dc, [2 dc in next dc, dc in each of next 3 dc] 11 times, join in top of beg ch-3. *(60 dc)*

Rnd 6: Ch 3, dc in first dc, dc in each of next 4 dc, [2 dc in next dc, dc in each of next 4 dc] 11 times, join in top of beg ch-3. *(72 dc)*

Rnd 7: Ch 3, dc in first dc, dc in each of next 5 dc, [2 dc in next dc, dc in each of next 5 dc] 11 times, join in top of beg ch-3. *(84 dc)*

Fasten off.

Eye
Make 2.

With black, ch 4, 3 dc in first ch. Fasten off. *(4 dc)*

Nose

Rep for Eye.

Mouth

Row 1: With black, ch 3, sl st in 2nd ch from hook and in next ch, ch 2, sl st in 2nd ch from hook and in last foundation ch, ch 17, sl st in 2nd ch from hook and in next ch, ch 2, sl st in 2nd ch from hook and in same ch as last sl st on ch-17. Leaving long end for sewing, fasten off.

Leaf
Make 2.

Row 1: With green, ch 4, 2 sc in first ch, turn. *(2 sc)*

Row 2: Ch 3, 2 sc in first sc, sc in next sc, turn. *(3 sc)*

Rows 3–6: Ch 3, 2 sc in first sc, sc in each of next 2 sc, turn. *(4 sc)*

Row 7: Ch 3, 2 sc in first sc, sc in next sc, turn. *(3 sc)*

Row 8: Ch 3, sc in first sc, sc in next sc, turn. *(2 sc)*

Row 9: Ch 3, sc in first sc, sl st in next sc. Leaving long end for sewing, fasten off. *(1 sc)*

FALL

Stem

Row 1: With brown, ch 8, 2 dc in 4th ch from hook (*sk chs count as first dc*), dc in each of next 3 ch, 2 dc in last ch, turn. *(8 dc)*

Row 2: Ch 3, dc in first dc, dc in each of next 5 dc, **dc dec** *(see Stitch Guide)* in last 2 dc. Leaving long end for sewing, fasten off. *(8 sts)*

Finishing

With long ends and tapestry needle, sew Mouth, Eyes, Nose, Leaves and Stem to Pumpkin as shown in photo. ●

School Bus

Design by Linda K. Kahle

Skill Level

 EASY

Finished Measurements

9 inches wide x 7 inches long, excluding Wheels

Materials

- Medium (worsted) weight cotton yarn:
  2 oz/100 yds/60g yellow
  1 oz/50 yds/30g black
  ½ oz/25 yds/15g red
- Sizes E/4/3.5mm and I/9/5.5mm crochet hooks
- Tapestry needle
- White cotton thread

Gauge

Gauge is not important for this project.

Pattern Note

Join with slip stitch as indicated unless otherwise stated.

Special Stitch

Top stitch (top st): Holding yarn at back of work, insert hook between sts, yo, pull lp through st and lp on hook.

Bus

Row 1 (WS): Beg at top with yellow and size I hook, ch 26, sc in 2nd ch from hook and in each rem ch across, turn. *(25 sc)*

Rows 2–11: Ch 1, sc in each sc across, turn.

Row 12: Ch 7, sc in 2nd ch from hook and in each of next 5 chs, sc in each rem sc across, turn. *(31 sc)*

Rows 13–24: Ch 1, sc in each sc across, turn.

Designer Tip

Make a 2nd set of Windows, Wheels and Top Lights and apply them to the back of the Bus to make your dishcloth reversible. Don't forget the top stitching!

At end of last row, do not fasten off.

Edging

Rnd 1: With RS facing, ch 1, sc evenly around Bus, working 3 sc in each corner, **join** *(see Pattern Note)* in first sc. Fasten off.

Window
Make 3.

Row 1: With black and size I hook, ch 5, sc in 2nd ch from hook and in each rem ch across, turn. *(4 sc)*

Rows 2–4: Ch 1, sc in each sc across, turn.

Leaving long end for sewing, fasten off at end of last row.

Wheel
Make 2.

Rnd 1 (RS): With black and size I hook, ch 4, 11 dc in first ch *(sk chs count as first dc)*, join in top of beg ch-4. *(12 dc)*

Rnd 2: Ch 1, 2 sc in first st and in each rem st around, join in first sc. Leaving long tail for sewing, fasten off. *(24 sc)*

Stop Sign
Rnds 1 & 2: With red and size E hook, rep rnds 1 and 2 as for Wheel.

Top Light
Make 2.

Rnd 1 (RS): With red and size E hook, ch 2, 12 dc in first ch, join in top of first dc. Leaving long end for sewing, fasten off. *(12 dc)*

Finishing

With RS facing and black, **top st** *(see Special Stitch)* across between rows 9 and 10 and between rows 10 and 11. With white thread, using **backstitch** *(see illustration)* embroider the word "STOP" on Stop Sign.

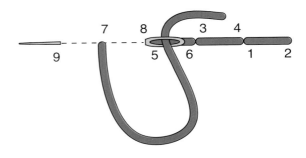

Backstitch

Position Windows, Stop Sign, Wheels and Top Lights on Bus and sew in place as shown in photo. ●

Before the Pie

Design by Maggie Weldon

Skill Level

 EASY

Finished Measurements

7¼ inches wide x 8 inches long, excluding Stem and Leaves

Materials

- Medium (worsted) weight cotton yarn:
  1½ oz/75 yds/45g red
  ½ oz/25 yds/15g each green and brown
- Size H/8/5mm crochet hook
- Tapestry needle

4 MEDIUM

Gauge

Gauge is not important for this project.

Pattern Note

Join with slip stitch as indicated unless otherwise stated.

Apple

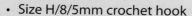

Row 1 (RS): Beg at bottom with red, ch 13, sc in 2nd ch from hook and in each rem ch across, turn. *(12 sc)*

Row 2: Ch 1, sc in each sc across, turn.

Row 3: Ch 1, 2 sc in first sc, sc in each rem sc across to last sc, 2 sc in last sc, turn. *(14 sc)*

Rows 4 & 5: [Rep row 3] twice. *(18 sc at end of row 5)*

Rows 6 & 7: [Rep row 2] twice.

Rows 8 & 9: [Rep row 3] twice. *(22 sc at end of row 9)*

Rows 10–20: [Rep row 2] 11 times.

Row 21: Rep row 3. *(24 sc)*

Rows 22–24: [Rep row 2] 3 times.

At end of last row, do not fasten off.

Top Right

Row 25: Ch 1, **sc dec** *(see Stitch Guide)* in first 2 sc, sc in each of next 7 sc, sc dec in next 2 sc, turn, leaving rem sc unworked. *(9 sts)*

Row 26: Ch 1, sc dec in first 2 sts, sc in each of next 5 sts, sc dec in last 2 sts, turn. *(7 sts)*

Row 27: Ch 1, sc dec in first 2 sts, sc in each of next 3 sts, sc dec in last 2 sts, **do not turn**. *(5 sts)*

Top Left

Row 1: Working along row ends of previous 3 rows, sl st in each row end across, working in unworked sts on row 24, sl st in each of next 2 sc, ch 1, sc dec in next 2 sc, sc in each of next 7 sc, sc dec in last 2 sc, turn. *(9 sc)*

Rows 2 & 3: Rep rows 26 and 27.

Edging
Rnd 1: With RS facing, ch 1, working along row ends, sc in each row end across, working across opposite side of foundation ch, 2 sc in first ch, hdc in next ch, 3 dc in next ch, hdc in next ch, sc in next ch, sl st in each of next 2 chs, sc in next ch, hdc in next ch, 3 dc in next ch, hdc in next ch, 2 sc in last ch, working along row ends, sc in each row end across, working across top of Apple, sc in each st across, **join** *(see Pattern Note)* in first sc. Fasten off.

Stem
With brown, ch 20, dc in 4th ch from hook and in each rem ch across. Leaving long end for sewing, fasten off. *(18 dc)*

Leaf
Row 1: With green, ch 15, sl st in 2nd ch from hook, *sc in next ch, hdc in next ch, dc in next ch, tr in next ch, 2 **dtr** *(see Stitch Guide)* in next ch, dtr in next ch, 2 dtr in next ch, tr in next ch, dc in next ch, hdc in next ch, sc in next ch*, (sl st, ch 1, sl st) in last ch, working across opposite side of foundation ch, rep from * to *, sl st in last ch. Leaving long end for sewing, fasten off.

Finishing
Fold Stem in half to form lp. Using long end, sew Stem to top of Apple as shown in photo. Sew 1 end of Leaf to Apple as shown in photo. ●

Breast Cancer Ribbon

Design by Linda K. Kahle

Skill Level
 EASY

Finished Measurement
9½ inches square

Materials
- Medium (worsted) weight cotton yarn:
  1 oz/50 yds/30g pink variegated
  ½ oz/25 yds/15g hot pink
- Size H/8/5mm crochet hook
- Tapestry needle

4 MEDIUM

Gauge
Gauge is not important for this project.

Pattern Notes
Chain-3 at beginning of row counts as first double crochet unless otherwise stated.

Join with slip stitch as indicated unless otherwise stated.

Special Stitch

Single crochet join (sc join): Place slip knot on hook, insert hook in indicated st, yo and draw up a lp, yo and draw through both lps on hook.

Dishcloth

Row 1 (RS): With pink variegated, ch 30, dc in 4th ch from hook *(sk chs count as first dc)* and in each rem ch across, turn. *(28 dc)*

Row 2: Ch 3 *(see Pattern Notes)*, dc in next dc and in each rem dc across, turn.

Rows 3–16: Rep row 2. Do not fasten off.

Edging

Rnd 1: Now working in rnds, ch 1, 3 sc in first dc, sc in next dc and in each rem dc across to last dc, 3 sc in last dc, working in row ends along side, work 26 sc evenly sp across, working across opposite side of foundation ch, 3 sc in first ch, sc in next ch and in each rem ch across to last ch, 3 sc in last ch, working in row ends along opposite side, work 26 sc evenly sp across, **join** *(see Pattern Notes)* in first sc. Fasten off.

Rnd 2: With RS facing, **sc join** *(see Special Stitch)* hot pink in any corner, ch 3, [sk next sc, sc in next sc, ch 3] around, join in first sc. Fasten off.

Ribbon

Row 1 (RS): With hot pink, ch 4, sc in 2nd ch from hook and in each of next 2 chs, turn. *(3 sc)*

Row 2: Ch 1, sc in each sc across, turn.

Rep row 2 until Ribbon measures 18 inches. Leaving long end for sewing, fasten off.

With RS facing, shape Ribbon in breast cancer sign and pin to front of Dishcloth. With long end and tapestry needle, sew Ribbon in place as shown in photo. ●

Illusions

Design by Carol Ballard

Skill Level

 EASY

Finished Measurements

9½ inches wide x 9 inches long

Materials

- Size 10 crochet cotton:
  2½ oz/125 yds/75g each
  white and black
  1 oz/50 yds/30g red
- Size E/4/3.5mm crochet hook
- Tapestry needle

0 LACE

Gauge

Gauge is not important for this project.

Pattern Notes

Hold 2 strands together unless otherwise stated.

Chain-3 at beginning of row counts as first double crochet unless otherwise stated.

Join with slip stitch as indicated unless otherwise stated.

Special Stitches

Single crochet join (sc join): Place slip knot on hook, insert hook in indicated st, yo and draw up a lp, yo and draw through both lps on hook.

Cluster (cl): Holding back last lp of each st on hook, 2 dc as indicated in instructions, yo, pull through 3 lps on hook.

Dishcloth

Row 1 (RS): With 2 strands white held tog *(see Pattern Notes)*, ch 43, sc in 2nd ch from hook and in each rem ch across, turn. *(42 sc)*

Row 2: Ch 1, sc in each of first 2 sc, hdc in each of next 2 sc, dc in each of next 2 sc, hdc in each of next 2 sc, [sc in each of next 2 sc, hdc in each of next 2 sc, dc in each of next 2 sc, hdc in each of next 2 sc] 4 times, sc in each of last 2 sc, **changing color** *(see Stitch Guide)* to black in last st, turn. Fasten off white.

Row 3: Ch 3 *(see Pattern Notes)*, dc in next sc, hdc in each of next 2 hdc, sc in each of next 2 dc, hdc in each of next 2 hdc, [dc in each of next 2 sc, hdc in each of next 2 hdc, sc in each of next 2 dc, hdc in each of next 2 hdc] 4 times, dc in each of last 2 sc, changing color to white in last st, turn. Fasten off black.

Row 4: Ch 1, turn, sc in each of first 2 dc, hdc in each of next 2 hdc, dc in each of next 2 sc, hdc in each of next 2 hdc, [sc in each of next 2 dc, hdc in each of next 2 hdc, dc in each of next 2 sc, hdc in each of next 2 hdc] 4 times, sc in each of last 2 dc, changing color to black in last st, turn. Fasten off white.

Rows 5–26: [Rep rows 3 and 4 alternately] 11 times.

At end of last row, fasten off.

Edging

Rnd 1: With RS facing and red, **sc join** *(see Special Stitches)* in last sc worked on last row, working across last row, sc in next st and in each rem st across to last sc, 2 sc in last sc, working in row ends along side, [2 sc in each dc row, sc in each sc row] across, working in opposite side of foundation ch, 2 sc in first ch, sc in next ch and in each rem ch across to last ch, 2 sc in last ch, working in row ends on opposite side, [sc in each sc row, 2 sc in each dc row] across, sc in same st as first sc, **join** *(see Pattern Notes)* in first sc.

Rnd 2: Ch 1, (sc, ch 2, **cl**—*see Special Stitches*) in first sc, sk next sc, [(sc, ch 2, cl) in next sc, sk next sc] around, join in first sc. Fasten off. ●

Fancy Heart

Design by Jeanne O'Bryan

Skill Level

 EASY

Finished Measurements

10 inches wide x 9½ inches long

Materials

- Medium (worsted) weight cotton yarn:
    1 oz/50 yds/30g pink
    ½ oz/25 yds/15g white
- Size H/8/5mm crochet hook
- Tapestry needle

Gauge

Gauge is not important for this project.

Pattern Notes

Chain-4 at beginning of row counts as first treble crochet unless otherwise stated.

Join with slip stitch as indicated unless otherwise stated.

Special Stitches

Cluster (cl): Holding back last lp of each st on hook, 4 dc as indicated in instructions *(5 lps on hook)*, yo, pull through all lps on hook.

Single crochet join (sc join): Place slip knot on hook, insert hook in indicated st, yo and draw up a lp, yo and draw through both lps on hook.

Picot: Ch 3, sl st in 3rd ch from hook.

Heart

Row 1 (RS): Beg at bottom with pink, ch 6, 3 dc in 5th ch from hook *(sk chs count as first tr)*, tr in last ch, turn. *(2 tr, 3 dc)*

Row 2: Ch 4 *(see Pattern Notes)*, dc in first tr, sk next dc, dc in next dc, ch 3, **cl** *(see Special Stitches)* around last dc made, ch 1, (dc, tr) in last tr, turn. *(1 cl)*

Row 3: Ch 4, 2 dc in first tr, dc in next dc, ch 2, sc in next ch-3 sp, ch 2, dc in next dc, (2 dc, tr) in last tr, turn. *(2 tr, 6 dc, 2 ch-2 sps, 1 sc)*

Row 4: Ch 4, 2 dc in first tr, sk next 2 dc, dc in next dc, ch 3, cl around last dc made, ch 1, sk next ch, dc in next ch, dc in next sc, dc in next ch, sk next ch, dc in next dc, ch 3, cl around last dc made, ch 1, sk next 2 dc, (2 dc, tr) in last tr, turn. *(2 tr, 7 dc, 2 ch-3 sps, 2 cls)*

Row 5: Ch 4, 2 dc in first tr, dc in each of next 2 dc, ch 2, sc in next ch-3 sp, ch 2, dc in each of next 3 dc, ch 2, sc in next ch-3 sp, ch 2, dc in each of next 2 dc, (2 dc, tr) in last tr, turn. *(2 tr, 11 dc, 4 ch-2 sps, 2 sc)*

Row 6: Ch 4, 2 dc in first tr, sk next dc, dc in next dc, ch 3, cl around last dc made, ch 1, sk next 2 dc, sk next ch, dc in next ch, dc in next sc, dc in next ch, sk next ch, sk next dc, dc in next dc, ch 3, cl around last dc made, ch 1, sk next dc, sk next ch, dc in next ch, dc

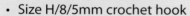

in next sc, dc in next ch, sk next ch, sk next 2 dc, dc in next dc, ch 3, cl around last dc made, ch 1, sk next dc, (2 dc, tr) in last tr, turn. *(2 tr, 10 dc, 3 ch-3 sps, 3 cls)*

Row 7: Ch 4, 2 dc in first tr, dc in each of next 2 dc, [ch 2, sc in next ch-3 sp, ch 2, dc in each of next 3 dc] twice, ch 2, sc in next ch-3 sp, ch 2, dc in each of next 2 dc, (2 dc, tr) in last tr, turn. *(2 tr, 14 dc, 6 ch-2 sps, 3 sc)*

Row 8: Ch 1, dc in first tr, dc in each of next 2 dc, sk next dc, dc in next dc, ch 3, cl around last dc made, ch 1, sk next ch, [dc in next ch, dc in next sc, dc in next ch, sk next ch, sk next dc, dc in next dc, ch 3, cl around last dc made, ch 1, sk next dc] twice, sk next ch, dc in next ch, dc in next sc, dc in next ch, sk next ch, dc in next dc, ch 3, cl around last dc made, ch 1, sk next dc, dc in each of next 2 dc, dc in last tr, turn. *(12 dc, 3 ch-3 sps, 4 cls)*

Row 9: Ch 1, dc in first dc, dc in next dc, *ch 2, sc in next ch-3 sp, ch 2, dc in each of next 3 dc, rep from * twice, ch 2, sc in next ch-3 sp, ch 2, dc in each of last 2 dc, turn. *(13 dc, 8 ch-2 sps, 3 sc)*

Row 10: Ch 1, dc in first dc, dc in next dc, dc in each of next 2 chs, dc in next sc, sk next 2 chs, sk next dc, dc in next dc, ch 3, cl around last dc made, ch 1, sk next dc, sk next ch, dc in next ch, dc in next sc, dc in next ch, sk next ch, sk next dc, dc in next dc, ch 3, cl around last dc made, ch 1, sk next dc, sk next ch, dc in next ch, dc in next sc, dc in next ch, sk next ch, sk next dc, dc in next dc, ch 3, cl around last dc made, ch 1, sk next dc, sk next 2 chs, dc in next sc, dc in each of next 2 chs, dc in each of next 2 dc, turn. *(16 dc, 3 ch-3 sps, 3 cls)*

Row 11: Ch 1, dc in first dc, dc in each of next 4 dc, [ch 2, sc in next ch-3 sp, ch 2, dc in each of next 3 dc] twice, ch 2, sc in next ch-3 sp, ch 2, dc in each of last 5 sts, turn. *(16 dc, 6 ch-2 sps, 3 sc)*

Shape First Lobe

Row 12: Ch 1, **dc dec** *(see Stitch Guide)* in first 2 dc, sk next dc, dc in next dc, ch 3, cl around last dc made, ch 1, sk next dc, sk next ch, dc in next ch, dc in next sc, dc in next ch, sk next ch, sk next dc, dc in next dc, ch 3, cl around last dc made, ch 1, sk next dc, dc dec

in next 2 chs, turn, leaving rem sts unworked. *(2 dc dec, 3 dc, 2 cls)*

Row 13: Ch 1, dc in first st, ch 1, sc in next ch-3 sp, ch 2, dc in each of next 3 dc, ch 2, sc in next ch-3 sp, ch 1, dc in last st, turn. *(5 dc, 2 ch-2 sps, 2 sc)*

Row 14: Ch 1, dc dec in first 2 sts, dc in next sc, sk next 2 chs, sk next dc, dc in next dc, ch 3, cl around last dc made, ch 1, sk next dc, sk next 2 chs, dc in next sc, dc dec in last 2 sts, turn. *(2 dc dec, 2 dc, 1 cl)*

Row 15: Ch 1, dc in first dc, sc in next ch-3 sp, dc in last dc. Fasten off. *(3 sts)*

2nd Lobe

Row 1: With WS facing, and working in unworked sts on row 11, sk first unworked sc, **join** *(see Pattern Notes)* pink in next ch, ch 2, dc in next ch, sk next dc, dc in next dc, ch 3, cl around last dc made, ch 1, sk next dc, sk next ch, dc in next ch, dc in next sc, dc in next ch, sk next ch, sk next dc, dc in next dc, ch 3, cl around last dc made, ch 1, sk next dc, dc dec in last 2 sts, turn. *(2 dc dec, 2 cls, 3 dc)*

Row 2: Ch 1, dc in first dc, ch 1, sc in next ch-3 sp, ch 2, dc in each of next 3 dc, ch 2, sc in next ch-3 sp, ch 1, dc in last st, turn. *(2 dc, 2 sc, 2 ch-2 sps)*

Row 3: Ch 1, dc dec in first dc and next ch, dc in next sc, sk next 2 chs, sk next dc, dc in next dc, ch 3, cl around last dc made, ch 1, sk next dc, sk next 2 chs, dc in next sc, dc dec in last 2 sts, turn. *(2 dc dec, 2 dc, 1 cl)*

Row 4: Ch 1, dc in first st, sc in next ch-3 sp, dc in last st. *(3 sts)*

Edging

Rnd 1: With RS facing, ch 1, sc evenly around Heart, join in first sc. Fasten off pink.

Rnd 2: With RS facing, **sc join** *(see Special Stitches)* white in center top sc *(between Lobes)*, [sc in next sc, **picot** *(see Special Stitches)*, sc in next sc] around, working 3 sc in bottom point of Heart, join in first sc. Fasten off. ●

Penguin

Design by Kathleen Stuart

Skill Level

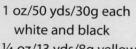 EASY

Finished Measurements

5½ inches wide x 10 inches long, excluding Feet

Materials

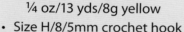

- Medium (worsted) weight cotton yarn:
  1 oz/50 yds/30g each white and black
  ¼ oz/13 yds/8g yellow
- Size H/8/5mm crochet hook
- Tapestry needle
- Stitch marker

Gauge

Gauge is not important for this project.

Pattern Notes

Join with slip stitch as indicated unless otherwise stated.

Chain-2 at beginning of round counts as first half double crochet unless otherwise stated.

Chain-3 at beginning of round counts as first double crochet unless otherwise stated.

Special Stitch

Single crochet join (sc join): Place slip knot on hook, insert hook in indicated st, yo and draw up a lp, yo and draw through both lps on hook.

Penguin

Body

Rnd 1 (RS): With white, ch 18, 3 dc in 4th ch from hook (*sk chs count as first dc*), dc in each of next 13 chs, 8 dc in last ch, working across opposite side of foundation ch, dc in each of next 13 chs, 4 dc in last ch, **join** (*see Pattern Notes*) in first dc. (*42 dc*)

Rnd 2: Ch 1, 2 sc in same dc as joining, 2 sc in each of next 2 dc, sc in each of next 5 dc, hdc in next dc, dc in each of next 9 dc, 2 dc in each of next 6 dc, dc in each of next 9 dc, hdc in next dc, sc in each of next 5 dc, 2 sc in each of last 3 dc, join in first sc. (*54 sts*)

Rnd 3: Ch 1, 2 sc in same st as joining, 2 sc in each of next 3 sts, sc in each of next 10 sts, hdc in next st, dc in each of next 8 sts, 2 dc in each of next 8 sts, dc in each of next 8 sts, hdc in next st, sc in each of next 10 sts, 2 sc in each of last 4 sts, join in first sc. Fasten off. (*70 sts*)

Rnd 4: With RS facing, join black in same st as joining, **ch 2** (*see Pattern Notes*), hdc in same st, [hdc in next st, 2 hdc in next st] twice, hdc in each of next 13 sts, sc in next st, dc in each of next 10 sts, [2 dc in next st, dc in next st] 6 times, dc in each of next 10 sts, sc in next st, hdc in each of next 12 sts, [2 hdc in next st, hdc in next st] 3 times, join in top of beg ch-2. (*82 sts*)

Rnd 5: Ch 3 (*see Pattern Notes*), dc in each of next 19 sts, hdc in next st, sc in next st, hdc in next st, dc in each of next 14 sts, [2 dc in next st, dc in next st] 5 times, dc in each of next 12 sts, hdc in next st, sc in next st, hdc in next st, dc in each of last 20 sts, join in top of beg ch-3. Place marker in 47th st. Fasten off. (*87 sts*)

Feet

Row 1: With WS facing, **sc join** (see Special Stitch) yellow in marked st, sc in each of next 6 dc, turn, leaving rem sts unworked. (7 sc)

Row 2: Ch 1, sc in first sc, *ch 3, sc in 2nd ch from hook, sc in next ch, sc in next sc on row 1 (first toe made), ch 4, sc in 2nd ch from hook, sc in each of next 2 chs, sc in next sc on row 1 (long toe made), ch 3, sc in 2nd ch from hook, sc in next ch, sc in next sc on row 1 (next toe made), rep from * once. Fasten off.

Top Beak

Row 1 (RS): With yellow, ch 4, sc in 2nd ch from hook and in each rem ch across, turn. (3 sc)

Row 2: Ch 1, sk first sc, sc in each of next 2 sc, turn. (2 sc)

Row 3: Ch 1, **sc dec** (see Stitch Guide) in first 2 sc. Fasten off. (1 st)

Bottom Beak

Row 1: With RS of Top Beak facing and working across opposite side of foundation ch, sc join yellow in first ch, sc in each of next 2 chs, turn. (3 sc)

Rows 2 & 3: Rep rows 2 and 3 of Top Beak. At end of last row, do not fasten off.

Beak Edging

Rnd 1: With RS facing, working in row ends along side, sc evenly sp across to row 3 of Top Beak, (sc, ch 2, sc) in st on row 3, working in row ends along opposite side, sc evenly across to row 3 of Bottom Beak, (sc, ch 2, sc) in st on row 3 of Bottom Beak, join in first sc. Fasten off.

Finishing

With RS of Penguin facing and working across foundation ch, sew Beak on Penguin as shown in photo, leaving remainder of each Beak unsewn as show in photo. With black and tapestry needle, embroider eyes using **satin stitch** (see illustration) above Beak as shown in photo. ●

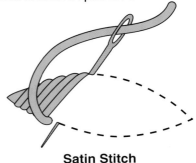

Satin Stitch

Gingerbread House

Design by Maggie Weldon

Skill Level

 ■■□□ EASY

Finished Measurements

8½ inches wide x 9 inches long

Materials

- Medium (worsted) weight cotton yarn:
  1½ oz/75 yds/45g brown
  1 oz/50 yds/30g white
  ¼ oz/13 yds/8g each red and orange/green/yellow/pink variegated
- Size H/8/5mm crochet hook
- Tapestry needle

Gauge

Gauge is not important for this project.

Pattern Notes

Chain-1 at beginning of row loosely to avoid curling on edges.

Join with slip stitch unless otherwise stated.

To change color, work stitch with old color to last yarn over, drop old color, yarn over with new color and draw through all lps on hook to finish stitch. Leave old color until next needed.

Dishcloth

House

Row 1 (RS): With brown, ch 30, sc in 2nd ch from hook, [dc in next ch, sc in next ch] across, turn. *(29 sts)*

Row 2: Ch 1 *(see Pattern Notes)*, dc in first sc, [sc in next dc, dc in next sc] across, turn.

Row 3: Ch 1, sc in first dc, [dc in next sc, sc in next dc] across, turn.

Rows 4–13: [Rep rows 2 and 3 alternately] 5 times.

Row 14: Rep row 2.

Roof Shaping

Row 15: Ch 1, sk first dc, sk next sc, [sc in next dc, dc in next sc] across to last 3 sts, sk next 2 sts, sc in last st, turn. *(25 sts)*

Row 16: Ch 1, sk first sc, sk next dc, [dc in next sc, sc in next dc] across to last 3 sts, sk next 2 sts, dc in last st, turn. *(21 sts)*

Row 17: Rep row 15. *(17 sts)*

Row 18: Ch 1, sk first sc, [sc in next dc, dc in next sc] across to last 2 sts, sk next sc, sc in next dc, turn. *(15 sts)*

Rows 19–24: [Rep row 18] 6 times. At end of row 24, fasten off. *(3 sts)*

Frosting

Row 1: With white, *ch 6, sl st in 2nd ch from hook, sl st in next ch, sk next 2 chs, 2 dc in first ch* *(icicle made)*, rep from * to * 4 times, ch 5 *(for peak)*, rep from * to * 5 times, turn. *(10 icicles)*

Row 2: Ch 1, working in first icicle, 2 hdc in top of last dc worked, hdc in side of same dc, hdc in first ch of ch-6 of same icicle, *working in next icicle, hdc in top of next dc, hdc in side of same dc, hdc in first ch of ch-6 of same icicle*; rep from * to * 3 times, hdc in each of next 2 chs, 3 hdc in next ch, hdc in each of next 2 chs, rep from * to * 5 times, hdc in same st as last hdc, turn. *(39 hdc)*

Row 3: Ch 1, hdc in each hdc, across, working 3 hdc in center hdc of 3-hdc group, turn.

Row 4: Ch 1, sc in each hdc across, working 2 sc in center hdc of 3-hdc group. Fasten off.

Front Door

With white, ch 30. Leaving long end for sewing, fasten off.

Window

Rnd 1: With white, ch 8, [dc in first ch, ch 4] 3 times, **join** *(see Pattern Notes)* in 5th ch of beg ch-8. Finish off, leaving long end.

Candy
Make 6.

With variegated, ch 2, 8 sc in 2nd ch from hook, join in first sc. Leaving long end for sewing, fasten off.

Right-Facing Candy Cane
With red, ch 16, 2 sc in 2nd ch from hook, ***change color** (see Pattern Notes) to white, with white, 2 sc in next ch, change color to red, with red, 2 sc in next ch, rep from * twice; [change color to white, with white, sc in each of next 2 chs, change color to red, with red, sc in each of next 2 chs] twice. Leaving long end for sewing, fasten off.

Left-Facing Candy Cane
With red, ch 16, sc in 2nd ch from hook, sc in next ch, change color to white, with white, sc in each of next 2 chs, change color to red, with red, sc in each of next 2 chs, change color to white, with white, sc in each of next 2 chs, change color to red, with red, 2 sc in next ch, *change color to white, with white, 2 sc in next ch, change color to red, with red, 2 sc in next ch, rep from * twice. Leaving long end for sewing, fasten off.

Finishing
With RS facing, sew Frosting on House as shown in photo.

Using long ends and tapestry needle, sew Door and Window on House. With white, embroider **French knot** (see illustration) on Door for doorknob.

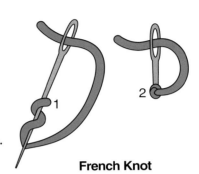

French Knot

Using long ends and tapestry needle, sew Candy on Frosting and Candy Canes on either side of Front Door as shown in photo. ●

Snowman
Design by Maggie Weldon

Skill Level
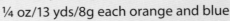 EASY

Finished Measurements
Face: 8½ inches in diameter

Snowman: 9¾ inches long, including Hat

Materials
- Medium (worsted) weight cotton yarn:
    1½ oz/75 yds/45g white
    1 oz/50 yds/30g black
    ¼ oz/13 yds/8g each orange and blue
- Size H/8/5mm crochet hook
- Tapestry needle

4 MEDIUM

Gauge

Gauge is not important for this project.

Pattern Notes

Chain-3 at beginning of round counts as first double crochet unless otherwise stated.

Join with slip stitch as indicated unless otherwise stated.

Special Stitch

Single crochet join (sc join): Place slip knot on hook, insert hook in indicated st, yo and draw up a lp, yo and draw through both lps on hook.

Dishcloth

Snowman

Face

Rnd 1 (RS): With white, ch 4, sl st in first ch to form ring, **ch 3** (see Pattern Notes), 11 dc in ring, **join** (see Pattern Notes) in top of beg ch-3. (12 dc)

Rnd 2: Ch 3, dc in same st as joining, 2 dc in each rem dc around, join in top of beg ch-3. (24 dc)

Rnd 3: Ch 3, dc in same dc as joining, dc in next dc, [2 dc in next dc, dc in next dc] around, join in top of beg ch-3. (36 dc)

Rnd 4: Ch 3, dc in same dc as joining, dc in each of next 2 dc, [2 dc in next dc, dc in each of next 2 dc] around, join in top of beg ch-3. (48 dc)

Rnd 5: Ch 3, dc in same dc as joining, dc in each of next 3 dc, [2 dc in next dc, dc in each of next 3 dc] around, join in top of beg ch-3. (60 dc)

Rnd 6: Ch 3, dc in same dc as joining, dc in each of next 4 dc, [2 dc in next dc, dc in each of next 4 dc] around, join in top of beg ch-3. (72 dc)

Rnd 7: Ch 3, dc in same dc as joining, dc in each of next 5 dc, [2 dc in next dc, dc in each of next 5 dc] around, join in top of beg ch-3. Fasten off. (84 dc)

Hat

Row 1 (RS): Beg at brim with black, ch 27, sc in 2nd ch from hook and in each rem ch across, turn. (26 sc)

Rows 2 & 3: Ch 1, sc in each sc across, turn.

At end of row 3, fasten off black.

Row 4: With RS facing, sk first 4 sc, **sc join** (see Special Stitch) blue in 5th sc, sc in each of next 17 sc, turn, leaving rem sts unworked. (18 sc)

Row 5: Ch 1, sc in each sc across. Fasten off blue.

Row 6: With RS facing, sc join black in first sc of row 5, sc in each sc across, turn.

Row 7: Ch 1, 2 sc in first sc, sc in each rem sc across to last sc, 2 sc in last sc, turn. (20 sc)

Row 8: Rep row 7. Fasten off. (22 sc)

Eye
Make 2.

Rnd 1: With black, ch 2, 6 sc in 2nd ch from hook, join in first sc. Leaving long end for sewing, fasten off. (6 sc)

Mouth

With black, ch 3, sl st in 2nd ch from hook and in next ch, ch 2, sl st in 2nd ch from hook and in last foundation ch, ch 21, sl st in 2nd ch from hook and in next ch, ch 2, sl st in 2nd ch from hook and in same ch as last sl st on ch-17. Leaving long end for sewing, fasten off.

Carrot

With orange, ch 6, sl st in 2nd ch from hook, sl st in next ch, sc in each of next 2 chs, (2 sc, sl st) in last ch, working across opposite side of foundation ch, sl st in each of next 4 chs. Leaving long end for sewing, fasten off.

Finishing

Sew Hat to top of Face as shown in photo. Using long ends and tapestry needle, sew Eyes, Carrot and Mouth on Face. ●

Rudolph

Design by Kathleen Stuart

Skill Level

■■□□ EASY

Finished Measurements

5¼ inches wide x 9½ inches tall, excluding Antlers

Materials

- Medium (worsted) weight cotton yarn:
  - 2 oz/100 yds/60g brown
  - ½ oz/25 yds/15g off-white
  - ¼ oz/13 yds/8g each red, white and black
- Size H/8/5mm crochet hook
- Tapestry needle

 **4 MEDIUM**

Gauge

Gauge is not important for this project.

Pattern Notes

Join with slip stitch as indicated unless otherwise stated.

Chain-2 at beginning of row or round counts as first half double crochet unless otherwise stated.

Chain-3 at beginning of round counts as first double crochet unless otherwise stated.

Special Stitch

Picot: Ch 3, sl st in 3rd ch from hook.

Dishcloth

Head

Rnd 1 (RS): With brown, ch 18, 3 dc in 4th ch from hook (*sk chs count as first dc*), dc in each of next 13 chs, 8 dc in last ch, working across opposite side of foundation ch, dc in each of next 13 chs, 4 dc in same ch as first 3 dc, **join** (*see Pattern Notes*) in 3rd ch of sk chs. (*42 dc*)

Rnd 2: Ch 1, 2 sc in same dc as joining, 2 sc in each of next 2 dc, sc in each of next 5 dc, hdc in next dc, dc in each of next 9 dc, 2 dc in each of next 6 dc, dc in each of next 9 dc, hdc in next dc, sc in each of next 5 dc, 2 sc in each of last 3 dc, join in first sc. (*54 sts*)

Rnd 3: Ch 1, 2 sc in same st, 2 sc in each of next 3 sts, sc in each of next 10 sts, hdc in next st, dc in each of next 8 sts, 2 dc in each of next 8 sts, dc in each of next 8 sts, hdc in next st, sc in each of next 10 sts, 2 sc in each of last 4 sts, join in first sc. (*70 sts*)

Rnd 4: Ch 2 (*see Pattern Notes*), hdc in same st, [hdc in next st, 2 hdc in next st] twice, hdc in each of next 13 sts, sc in next st, dc in each of next 10 sts, [2 dc in next st, dc in next st] 6 times, dc in each of next 10 sts, sc in next st, hdc in each of next 12 sts, [2 hdc in next st, hdc in next st] 3 times, join in top of beg ch-2. *(82 sts)*

Rnd 5: Ch 3 *(see Pattern Notes)*, dc in each of next 19 sts, hdc in next st, sc in next st, hdc in next st, dc in each of next 14 sts, [2 dc in next st, dc in next st] 5 times, dc in each of next 12 sts, hdc in next st, sc in next st, hdc in next st, dc in each of last 20 sts, join in top of beg ch-3. Fasten off. *(87 sts)*

Antler
Make 2.

Row 1 (RS): With off-white, ch 10, sl st in 2nd ch from hook, sl st in each of next 5 chs *(leave rem 3 chs unworked)*, ch 10, sl st in 2nd ch from hook, sl st in next 5 chs *(leave rem 3 chs unworked)*, ch 6, sl st in 2nd ch from hook, sl st in next 4 chs, sl st in each of 6 unworked chs, turn.

Row 2: Ch 2, working in unused lps on opposite side of ch sts and in each sl st, hdc around shape, working 5 hdc in each Antler tip. Fasten off.

Ear
Make 2.

Rnd 1 (RS): With brown, ch 6, 3 hdc in 3rd ch from hook *(sk chs count as first hdc)*, hdc in each of next 2

chs, (4 hdc, **picot**—*see Special Stitch*, 4 hdc) in last ch, working across opposite side of foundation ch, hdc in each of next 2 chs, 4 hdc in last ch, join in 3rd ch of sk chs. Leaving long end for sewing, fasten off.

Nose
Rnd 1 (RS): With red, ch 2, 6 sc in 2nd ch from hook, join in first sc. *(6 sc)*

Rnd 2: Ch 2, hdc in same st, 2 hdc in each rem sc around, join in top of beg ch-2. Leaving long end for sewing, fasten off. *(12 hdc)*

Eye
Make 2.

Rnd 1 (RS): With black, ch 2, 6 sc in 2nd ch from hook, **changing color** *(see Stitch Guide)* to white in last sc. Fasten off black. *(6 sc)*

Row 2: With white, ch 1, 2 sc in each of next 4 sc, sl st in next sc. Leaving long end for sewing, fasten off.

Finishing
With long ends and tapestry needle, sew Antlers, Ears, Nose and Eyes on Head as shown in photo. ●

Snowflake

Design by Maggie Weldon

Skill Level
 EASY

Finished Measurements
Snowflake: 6¼ inches point to point

Dishcloth: 10¼ inches point to point

Materials
- Medium (worsted) weight cotton yarn:
  1 oz/50 yds/30g each white and blue
- Size H/8/5mm crochet hook
- Tapestry needle

Gauge

Gauge is not important for this project.

Pattern Notes

Chain-5 at beginning of round counts as first double crochet and chain-2 space unless otherwise stated.

Join with slip stitch as indicated unless otherwise stated.

Chain-4 at beginning of round counts as first double crochet and chain-1 space unless otherwise stated.

Special Stitches

Beginning shell (beg shell): Ch 3, (dc, ch 2, 2 dc) in indicated st or sp.

Shell (shell): (2 dc, ch 2, 2 dc) in indicated st or sp.

Single crochet join (sc join): Place slip knot on hook, insert hook in indicated st, yo and draw up a lp, yo and draw through both lps on hook.

Large picot (lg picot): Ch 4, sl st in 3rd ch from hook, ch 1 as indicated in instructions.

V-stitch (V-st): (Dc, ch 1, dc) in indicated st or sp.

Beginning cluster (beg cl): Ch 3, holding last lp of each st on hook, 2 dc in same st or sp as indicated, yo, draw through 4 lps on hook.

Small picot (sm picot): Ch 3, sl st in last st worked as indicated in instructions.

Cluster (cl): Holding last lp of each st on hook, 3 dc in same st or sp as indicated, yo, draw through 4 lps on hook.

Dishcloth

Rnd 1 (RS): With blue, ch 4, sl st in first ch to form ring, **ch 5** *(see Pattern Notes)*, [2 dc in ring, ch 2] 5 times, dc in ring, **join** *(see Pattern Notes)* in 3rd ch of beg ch-5. *(12 dc, 6 ch-2 sps)*

Rnd 2: Sl st in next corner ch-2 sp, **beg shell** *(see Special Stitches)* in same sp, ch 1, [**shell** *(see Special Stitches)* in next ch-2 sp, ch 1] around, join in top of beg ch-3. *(6 shells, 6 ch-1 sps)*

Rnd 3: Sl st in next dc, sl st in next ch-2 sp, beg shell in same sp, ch 1, 2 dc in next ch-1 sp, ch 1, [shell in next corner ch-2 sp, ch 1, 2 dc in next ch-1 sp, ch 1] around, join in top of beg ch-3. *(6 shells, 12 ch-1 sps, 12 dc)*

Rnd 4: Sl st in next dc, sl st in next ch-2 sp, beg shell in same sp, ch 1, [2 dc in next ch-1 sp, ch 1] twice, *shell in next corner ch-2 sp, ch 1, [2 dc in next ch-1 sp, ch 1] twice, rep from * around, join in top of beg ch-3. *(6 shells, 18 ch-1 sps, 24 dc)*

Rnd 5: Sl st in next dc, sl st in next ch-2 sp, beg shell in same sp, ch 1, [2 dc in next ch-1 sp, ch 1] 3 times, *shell in next corner ch-2 sp, ch 1, [2 dc in next ch-1 sp, ch 1] 3 times, rep from * around, join in top of beg ch-3. *(6 shells, 24 ch-1 sps, 36 dc)*

Rnd 6: Sl st in next dc, sl st in next ch-2 sp, beg shell in same sp, ch 1, [2 dc in next ch-1 sp, ch 1] 4 times, *shell in next corner ch-2 sp, ch 1, [2 dc in next ch-1 sp, ch 1] 4 times, rep from * around, join in top of beg ch-3. Fasten off. *(6 shells, 30 ch-1 sps, 48 dc)*

Edging

Rnd 1: With RS facing, **sc join** *(see Special Stitches)* white in any corner ch-2 sp, **lg picot** *(see Special Stitches)*, sc in same st, lg picot, [sc in next ch-1 sp, lg picot] across to next corner, *(sc, lg picot, sc) in next corner ch-2 sp, lg picot, [sc in next ch-1 sp, lg picot] across to next corner, rep from * around, join in first sc. Fasten off. *(42 sc, 42 lg picot)*

Snowflake

Rnd 1: With white, ch 2, 6 sc in 2nd ch from hook, join in first sc. *(6 sc)*

Rnd 2: Ch 4 *(see Pattern Notes)*, dc in same st, ch 1, [**V-st** *(see Special Stitches)* in next sc, ch 1] around, join in 3rd ch of beg ch-4. *(6 V-sts, 6 ch-1 sps)*

Rnd 3: Sl st in next ch-1 sp, **beg cl** *(see Special Stitches)* in same sp, ch 3, sc in next ch-1 sp, **sm picot** *(see Special Stitches)*, ch 3, ***cl** *(see Special Stitches)* in ch-1 sp of next V-st, ch 3, sc in next ch-1 sp, sm picot, ch 3, rep from * 4 times, join in top of beg cl.

Rnd 4: Ch 3, beg cl in same st as joining, sm picot, ch 5, sc in next picot, sm picot, ch 5, *cl in next cl, sm picot, ch 5, sc in next picot, sm picot, ch 5, rep from * 4 times, join in top of beg cl. Fasten off.

Finishing

With RS facing, sew Snowflake on front of Dishcloth, aligning points as shown in photo. ●

Santa

Design by Maggie Weldon

Skill Level
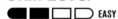 EASY

Finished Measurement
8½ inch in diameter, excluding Hat

Materials
- Medium (worsted) weight cotton yarn:
  1½ oz/75 yds/45g white
  1 oz/50 yds/30g red
  ½ oz/25 yds/15g pink
  ¼ oz/13 yds/8g black
- Size H/8/5mm crochet hook
- Tapestry needle

Gauge
Gauge is not important for this project.

Pattern Notes
Chain-3 at beginning of row counts as first double crochet unless otherwise stated.

Join with slip stitch as indicated unless otherwise stated.

Special Stitch
Single crochet join (sc join): Place slip knot on hook, insert hook in indicated st, yo and draw up a lp, yo and draw through both lps on hook.

Dishcloth

Face

Row 1 (RS): With pink, ch 4, sl st in first ch to form ring, **ch 3** (See Pattern Notes), 6 dc in ring, turn. (7 dc)

Row 2: Ch 3, dc in first dc, 2 dc in each of next 6 dc, turn. (14 dc)

Row 3: Ch 3, dc in first dc, dc in next dc, [2 dc in next dc, dc in next dc] 7 times. Fasten off pink. (21 dc)

Row 4: With WS facing, **sc join** (see Special Stitch) white in first dc, tr in same st, [(sc, tr) in next dc, sc in next dc, tr in next dc] 6 times, (sc, tr) in next dc, sc in last dc, turn. (29 sts)

Row 5: Ch 1, sc in each st across, turn.

Row 6: Ch 1, sc in first sc, [tr in next sc, sc in next sc] across, turn.

Row 7: Ch 1, 2 sc in first st, [sc in each of next 3 sts, 2 sc in next st] 7 times, turn. (37 sc)

Row 8: Rep row 6.

Row 9: Ch 1, 2 sc in first st, [sc in each of next 4 sts, 2 sc in next st] 7 times, sc in last sc, turn. (45 sc)

Row 10: Rep row 6.

Row 11: Ch 1, 2 sc in first st, [sc in each of next 5 sts, 2 sc in next st] 7 times, sc in each of last 2 sc, turn. (53 sc)

Row 12: Ch 1, sc in each sc across, do not turn.

Head

Row 1: Ch 1, with WS facing and working in row ends, sc in first white row end, [tr in next white row end, sc in next white row end] 4 times, (tr, sc) in each of next 3 pink row ends, tr in center ch, (tr, sc) in each of next 3 pink row ends, [tr in next white row end, sc in next white row end] 4 times, sc in last white row end, turn. (31 sts)

Row 2: Ch 1, **sc dec** (see Stitch Guide) in first 2 sc, sc in each rem sc across to last 2 sc, sc dec in last 2 sc, turn. (29 sc)

Row 3: Ch 1, sc in first st, [tr in next st, sc in next st] 14 times, turn.

Row 4: Ch 1, working in **back lps** (see Stitch Guide), [sc dec in next 2 sts] twice, sc in each rem st across to last 4 sts, [sc dec in next 2 sts] twice, turn. (25 sc)

Rows 5–10: Ch 1, sc dec in first 2 sts, sc in each rem st across to last 2 sts, sc dec in last 2 sts, turn. (13 sc at end of last row)

Edging

Rnd 1: Ch 1, with RS facing, work sc evenly sp around Face rows and in each sc of beard, **join** (see Pattern Notes) in first sc. Fasten off.

Moustache

Row 1: With white, ch 14, sc in 2nd ch from hook, [tr in next ch, sc in next ch] 6 times, turn. (13 sts)

Row 2: Ch 1, sc in each st across. Leaving long end for sewing, fasten off.

Nose

With pink, ch 2, 6 sc in 2nd ch from hook, join in first sc. Leaving long end for sewing, fasten off.

Eye
Make 2.

Rnd 1: With black, ch 2, 6 sc in 2nd ch from hook, join in first sc. Leaving long end for sewing, fasten off.

Hat

Row 1: With red, leaving 18-inch beg tail, ch 24, sc in 2nd ch from hook and in each rem ch across, turn. (23 sc)

Rows 2 & 3: Ch 1, sc dec in first 2 sc, sc in each rem sc across to last 2 sc, sc dec in last 2 sts, turn. (19 sc at end of row 3)

Row 4: Ch 1, sc in each sc across, turn.

Row 5: Rep row 2. *(17 sc)*

Rows 6–19: [Rep rows 4 and 5 alternately] 7 times. *(3 sts at end of row 19)*

Row 20: Ch 1, sc dec in first 2 sts, sc in next st, turn. *(2 sc)*

Row 21: Ch 1, sc dec in first 2 sts. Fasten off. *(1 sc)*

Pompom

Rnd 1: With white, ch 2, 6 sc in 2nd ch from hook, join in first sc. *(6 sc)*

Rnd 2: Ch 2, 2 sc in each sc around, join in first sc. Leaving long end for sewing, fasten off. *(12 sc)*

Finishing

With RS facing, using long end and tapestry needle, sew bottom of Hat across row 4 of Head. Fold point of Hat forward to brim. Working through all thicknesses, sew Pompom as shown in photo.

Using long ends and tapestry needle, sew Eyes and Moustache to Face. Sew Nose on center of Moustache. ●

Christmas Tree

Design by Carole Sisson

Skill Level
 EASY

Finished Measurements
7¼ inches wide at bottom x 8 inches long

Materials
- Medium (worsted) weight cotton yarn:
   1½ oz/75 yds/45g green
   ½ oz/25 yds/15g white
- Size G/6/4mm crochet hook
- Tapestry needle

4 MEDIUM

Gauge
Gauge is not important for this project.

Pattern Notes
Chain-4 at beginning of row counts as first double crochet and chain-1 space unless otherwise stated.

Join with slip stitch as indicated unless otherwise stated.

Special Stitch
Shell: (3 dc, ch 2, 3 dc) in sp as indicated in instructions.

Dishcloth

Tree Bottom

Row 1 (RS): Beg at base with green, ch 4, sl st in first ch to form ring, **ch 4** *(see Pattern Notes)*, **shell** *(see Special Stitch)* in ring, ch 1, dc in ring, turn. *(2 dc, 2 ch-1 sps, 1 shell)*

Row 2: Ch 4, 3 dc in first ch-1 sp, ch 1, shell in next ch-2 sp, ch 1, 3 dc in next ch-1 sp, ch 1, dc in last dc, turn. *(8 dc, 4 ch-1 sps, 1 shell)*

Row 3: Ch 4, 3 dc in first ch-1 sp, ch 1, 3 dc in next ch-1 sp, ch 1, shell in next ch-2 sp, ch 1, [3 dc in next ch-1 sp, ch 1] twice, dc in last dc, turn. *(14 dc, 5 ch-1 sps, 1 shell)*

Row 4: Ch 4, 3 dc in first ch-1 sp, ch 1, [3 dc in next ch-1 sp, ch 1] twice, shell in next ch-2 sp, ch 1, [3 dc in next ch-1 sp, ch 1] 3 times, dc in last dc, turn. *(20 dc, 7 ch-1 sps, 1 shell)*

Row 5: Ch 4, 3 dc in first ch-1 sp, ch 1, [3 dc in next ch-1 sp, ch 1] 3 times, shell in next ch-2 sp, ch 1, [3 dc in next ch-1 sp, ch 1] 4 times, dc in last dc, turn. *(26 dc, 8 ch-1 sps, 1 shell)*

Row 6: Ch 4, 3 dc in first ch-1 sp, ch 1, ch-1 sp, ch 1] 4 times, shell in next in next ch-1 sp, ch 1] 5 times, dc *(32 dc, 10 ch-1 sps, 1 shell)*

Treetop

Rows 1–4: Rep rows 1–4 of Tree Bottom.

Fasten off.

With RS facing, overlap Treetop with Tree Bottom as shown in photo. With green and tapestry needle and working through both thicknesses, sew Treetop to Tree Bottom.

Border

Rnd 1: With RS facing, **join** *(see Pattern Notes)* white in foundation ring on Tree Bottom, ch 4, (3 tr, ch 4, sl st) in ring *(tree trunk made)*, working in row ends along side, hdc evenly around entire Tree, working 3 hdc around outer branch points, sl st at inner branch joins, and 3 dc in ch-2 sp at top of Tree, join in first sl st. Fasten off. ●

White Snowflake

Design by Helen Gainsford

Skill Level

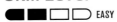 EASY

Finished Measurement

10 inches in diameter

Materials
- Medium (worsted) weight cotton yarn:
  2 oz/100 yds/60g white
- Size H/8/5mm crochet hook
- Tapestry needle

Gauge is not important for this project.

Pattern Notes

Join with slip stitch as indicated unless otherwise stated.

Chain-5 at beginning of round counts as first double crochet and chain-2 space unless otherwise stated.

Chain-3 at beginning of round counts as first double crochet unless otherwise stated.

Special Stitch

Picot: Ch 3, sl st in last sc made.

Dishcloth

Rnd 1 (RS): Ch 4, sl st in first ch to form ring, ch 1, 6 sc in ring, **join** (see Pattern Notes) in first sc. (6 sc)

Rnd 2: Ch 1, 2 sc in each sc around, join in first sc. (12 sc)

Rnd 3: Ch 5 (see Pattern Notes), [dc in next sc, ch 2] around, join in 3rd ch of beg ch-5. (12 dc, 12 ch-2 sps)

Rnd 4: Ch 3 (see Pattern Notes), dc in same st as joining, [2 dc in next ch-2 sp, dc in next dc, 2 dc in next ch-2 sp, 2 dc in next dc] 5 times, 2 dc in next ch-2 sp, dc in next dc, 2 dc in next ch-2 sp, join in top of beg ch-3. (42 dc)

Rnd 5: Ch 5, dc in next dc, ch 2, sk next dc, [dc in next dc, ch 2, dc in next dc, ch 2, sk next dc] around, join in 3rd ch of beg ch-5. (28 dc, 28 ch-2 sps)

Rnd 6: Ch 3, 2 dc in next ch-2 sp, [dc in next dc, 2 dc in next ch-2 sp] around, join in top of beg ch-3. (84 dc)

Rnd 7: Ch 1, sc in same st as joining, *sk next 2 dc, [dc, ch 1] 4 times in next dc, dc in same dc, sk next 2 dc**, sc in each of next 9 dc, rep from * around, ending last rep at **, sc in each of next 8 dc, join in first sc. (54 sc, 30 dc)

Rnd 8: Sl st in first dc, ch 1, sc in same st, **picot** (see Special Stitch), [sc in next ch-1 sp, sc in next dc, picot] 4 times, *sk next sc, sc in each of next 4 sc, ([picot] 3 times) in last sc made, sc in each of next 3 sc, sk next sc, sc in next dc, picot, [sc in next ch-1 sp, sc in next dc, picot] 4 times, rep from * 5 times, sk next sc, sc in each of next 4 sc, ([picot] 3 times) in last sc made, sc in each of next 3 sc, sk next sc, join in first sc. Fasten off. ●

Christmas Wreath

Design by Maggie Weldon

Skill Level

 EASY

Finished Measurement

8 inches in diameter

Materials

- Medium (worsted) weight cotton yarn:
    2 oz/100 yds/60g green
    1 oz/50 yds/30g white
    ½ oz/25 yds/15g red
- Size G/6/4mm crochet hook
- Tapestry needle

Gauge
Gauge is not important for this project.

Pattern Notes
Join with slip stitch as indicated unless otherwise stated.

Chain-3 at beginning of round counts as first double crochet unless otherwise stated.

Chain-5 at beginning of round counts as first double crochet and chain-2 space unless otherwise stated.

Special Stitch
Single crochet join (sc join): Place slip knot on hook, insert hook in indicated st, yo and draw up a lp, yo and draw through both lps on hook.

Wreath
Rnd 1 (RS): With white, ch 4 *(sk chs count as first dc)*, 11 dc in first ch, **join** *(see Pattern Notes)* in 3rd ch of beg ch-4. *(12 dc)*

Rnd 2: Ch 3 *(see Pattern Notes)*, dc in same st as joining, 2 dc in each rem dc around, join in top of beg ch-3. *(24 dc)*

Rnd 3: Ch 3, dc in same st as joining, dc in next dc, [2 dc in next dc, dc in next dc] around, join in top of beg ch-3. Fasten off. *(36 dc)*

Rnd 4: With RS facing, **sc join** *(see Special Stitch)* green in any dc, sc in each rem dc around, join in first sc. *(36 sc)*

Rnd 5: Ch 5 *(see Pattern Notes)*, sk next sc, [dc in next sc, ch 2, sk next dc] around, join in 3rd ch of beg ch-5. *(18 dc, 18 ch-2 sps)*

Rnd 6: Sl st in next ch-2 sp, ch 3, 2 dc in same sp, 4 dc in next ch-2 sp, *3 dc in each of next 2 ch-2 sps, 4 dc

in next ch-2 sp, rep from * around to last ch-2 sp, 3 dc in last ch-2 sp, join in top of beg ch-3. *(60 dc)*

Rnd 7: Ch 3, dc in same st as joining, dc in each of next 4 dc, [2 dc in next dc, dc in next 4 dc] around, join in top of beg ch-3. Fasten off. *(72 dc)*

Edging
With RS facing, sc join red in any dc, ch 4, sk next dc, [sc in next dc, ch 4, sk next dc] around, join in first sc. Fasten off.

Tie
With red, ch 100. Fasten off.

Finishing
Weave Tie through ch-2 sps on rnd 5 and tie in bow. ●

Snowman Block

Design by Maggie Weldon

Skill Level

 EASY

Finished Measurement

8½ inches square

Materials

- Medium (worsted) weight cotton yarn:
  - 1½ oz/75 yds/45g blue
  - 1 oz/50 yds/30g white
  - ½ oz/25 yds/15g black
  - ¼ oz/13 yds/8g orange
- Size H/8/5mm crochet hook
- Tapestry needle

Gauge

Gauge is not important for this project.

Pattern Note

Join with slip stitch as indicated unless otherwise stated.

Special Stitches

Single crochet join (sc join): Place slip knot on hook, insert hook in indicated st, yo and draw up a lp, yo and draw through both lps on hook.

Picot: Ch 3, sl st in 3rd ch from hook.

Dishcloth

Row 1 (RS): With blue, ch 26, sc in 2nd ch from hook and in each rem ch across, turn. *(25 sc)*

Rows 2 & 3: Ch 1, sc in each sc across, turn.

Rows 4–26: Referring to Color Chart, ch 1, sc in each sc across, turn.

Rows 27–29: Ch 1, sc in each sc across, turn.

Edging

Rnd 1: Ch 1, 3 sc in first sc and in each rem sc across to last sc, 3 sc in last sc, working in row ends along side, sc evenly across to corner, working across opposite side of foundation ch, 3 sc in first ch, sc in each rem ch across to last ch, 3 sc in last ch, working in row ends along opposite side, sc evenly across, **join** *(see Pattern Note)* in first sc. Fasten off.

Rnd 2: With RS facing, **sc join** *(see Special Stitches)* white in center sc of any corner 3-sc group, **picot** *(see Special Stitches)*, sc in same sc, [sk next sc, sc in next sc, picot] around, working (sc, picot, sc) in each corner, join in first sc.

Finishing

With orange and tapestry needle, using **satin stitch** *(see illustration)* embroider carrot shape for nose as shown in photo.

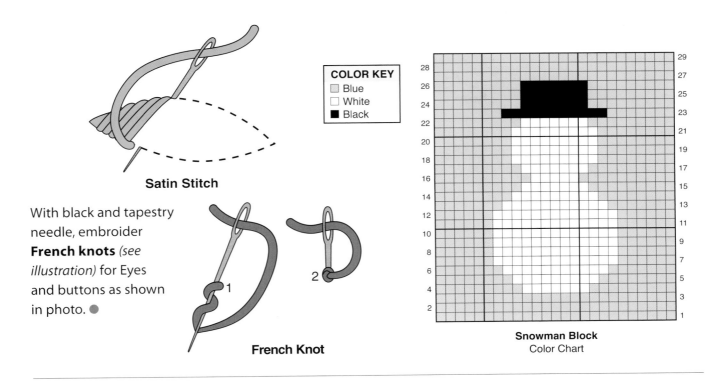

Satin Stitch

With black and tapestry needle, embroider **French knots** *(see illustration)* for Eyes and buttons as shown in photo. ●

1   2

French Knot

COLOR KEY
☐ Blue
☐ White
■ Black

Snowman Block
Color Chart

Poinsettia

Design by Maggie Weldon

Skill Level

■■☐☐ EASY

Finished Measurement

7¾ inches square

Materials

- Medium (worsted) weight cotton yarn:
  - 1 oz/50 yds/30g green
  - ½ oz/25 yds/15g each red and white
  - ¼ oz/13 yds/8g yellow
- Size H/8/5mm crochet hook
- Tapestry needle

4 MEDIUM

Gauge

Gauge is not important for this project.

Pattern Notes

Join with slip stitch as indicated unless otherwise stated.

Chain-4 at beginning of round counts as first double crochet and chain-1 space unless otherwise stated.

Chain-5 at beginning of round counts as first double crochet and chain-2 space unless otherwise stated.

Special Stitches

Puff stitch (puff st): Yo, insert hook in indicated st, yo, pull up lp to height of dc, [yo, insert hook in same st, yo, pull up lp to same height] 4 times, yo, draw through all 11 lps on hook.

Single crochet join (sc join): Place slip knot on hook, insert hook in indicated st, yo and draw up a lp, yo and draw through both lps on hook.

Dishcloth

Rnd 1 (RS): With yellow, ch 5, sl st in first ch to form ring, ch 1, 16 sc in ring, **join** *(see Pattern Notes)* in first sc. Fasten off yellow. *(16 sc)*

Rnd 2: With RS facing, join red in any sc, **ch 4** *(see Pattern Notes)*, [dc in next sc, ch 1] around, join in 3rd ch of beg ch-4. *(16 dc, 16 ch-1 sps)*

Rnd 3: Sl st in next ch-1 sp, ch 3, **puff st** *(see Special Stitches)* in same sp, ch 3, [puff st in next ch-1 sp, ch 3] around, join in top of first puff st. Fasten off red. *(16 puffs, 16 ch-3 sps)*

Rnd 4: With RS facing, **sc join** *(see Special Stitches)* white in any ch-3 sp, 2 sc in same sp, 3 sc in each of next 2 ch-3 sps, (hdc, dc, ch 2, dc, hdc) in next ch-3 sp, [3 sc in each of next 3 ch-3 sps, (hdc, dc, ch 2, dc, hdc) in next ch-3 sp] around, join in first sc. Fasten off white.

Rnd 5: With RS facing, join green in any corner ch-2 sp, **ch 5** *(see Pattern Notes)*, 2 dc in same sp, *dc in each rem st across to next corner, (2 dc, ch 2, 2 dc) in corner ch-2 sp, rep from * around, dc in first ch-2 sp, join in 3rd ch of beg ch-5.

Rnd 6: Sl st in ch-2 sp, ch 5, 2 dc in same sp, *dc in each rem dc across to corner, (2 dc, ch 2, 2 dc) in corner ch-2 sp, rep from * around, dc in first ch-2 sp, join in 3rd ch of beg ch-5. Fasten off green.

Rnd 7: With RS facing, sc join white in corner ch-2 sp, ch 2, sc in same sp, *sc in each rem dc around, (sc, ch 2, sc) in corner ch-2 sp, rep from * around, join in first sc. Fasten off white.

Rnd 8: With RS facing, sc join green in any ch-2 sp, ch 3, sc in same sp, ch 3, *[sk next sc, sc in next sc, ch 3] across to next corner ch-2 sp**, [sc, ch 3] twice in corner ch-2 sp, rep from * around, ending last rep at **, join in first sc. Fasten off. ●

Poinsettia in a Square

Design by Nancy Foutch

Skill Level
◼◼◻◻ EASY

Finished Measurement
7¾ inches square

Materials
- Medium (worsted) weight cotton yarn:
  2 oz/100 yds/60g each red and white
  ¼ oz/13 yds/8g each yellow and green
- Size G/6/4mm crochet hook
- Tapestry needle

Gauge

Gauge is not important for this project.

Pattern Notes

Join with slip stitch as indicated unless otherwise stated.

Chain-2 at beginning of row or round counts as first half double crochet unless otherwise stated.

Chain-3 at beginning of round counts as first double crochet unless otherwise stated.

Special Stitches

Beginning popcorn (beg pc): Ch 3, 2 dc in indicated st, drop lp from hook, insert hook from front to back in first dc made, pull dropped lp through st.

Popcorn (pc): 3 dc in indicated st, drop lp from hook, insert hook from front to back in first dc made, pull dropped lp through st.

Single crochet join (sc join): Place slip knot on hook, insert hook in indicated st, yo and draw up a lp, yo and draw through both lps on hook.

Dishcloth

Rnd 1 (RS): With yellow, ch 4, sl st in first ch to form ring, **beg pc** (see Special Stitches) in ring, ch 1, [**pc** (see Special Stitches) in ring, ch 1] 3 times, **join** (see Pattern Notes) in top of first pc. Fasten off yellow. (4 pc, 4 ch-1 sps)

Rnd 2: With RS facing, **sc join** (see Special Stitches) red in any ch-1 sp, ch 3, sc in next pc, ch 3, [sc in next ch-1 sp, ch 3, sc in next pc, ch 3] around, join in first sc. (8 sc, 8 ch-3 sps)

Rnd 3: Sl st in next ch-3 sp, **ch 2** (see Pattern Notes), (dc, tr, **picot**—see Special Stitches, tr, dc, hdc) in same sp, (hdc, dc, tr, picot, tr, dc, hdc) in each rem ch-3 sp around, join in top of beg ch-2. Fasten off red. (8 petals)

Rnd 4: With RS facing, sc join white in any picot, ch 6, [sc in next picot, ch 6] around, join in first sc. (8 sc, 8 ch-6 sps)

Rnd 5: Sl st in next ch-6 sp, **ch 3** (see Pattern Notes), (2 dc, ch 2, 3 dc) in same sp (corner made), 5 dc in next ch-6 sp, [(3 dc, ch 2, 3 dc) in next ch-6 sp (corner made), 5 dc in next ch-6 sp] around, join in top of beg ch-3. (44 dc, 4 ch-2 sps)

Rnd 6: Ch 3, dc in each rem dc around, working (3 dc, ch 2, 3 dc) in each corner ch-2 sp, join in top of beg ch-3. (68 dc)

Rnd 7: Rep rnd 6. Fasten off white. (92 dc)

Rnd 8: With RS facing, sc join red in any corner ch-2 sp, sc in same sp, sc in each rem dc around, working 2 sc in each corner ch-2 sp, join in first sc. Fasten off red.

Leaf

Row 1: With WS facing, working between petals on 1 side, join green in base of dc of first petal, ch 3, sl st in base of dc on next petal, turn.

Row 2: Ch 2, (dc, 2 tr, ch 3, sl st) in next ch-3 sp. Fasten off green.

Push Leaf between rnds to front of Dishcloth. ●

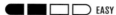
Candy Cane Blocks

Design by Maggie Weldon

Skill Level

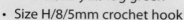 EASY

Finished Measurement

9½ inches square

Materials

- Medium (worsted) weight
  cotton yarn:
    1 oz/50 yds/30g each
    red and white
    ½ oz/25 yds/15g green
- Size H/8/5mm crochet hook
- Tapestry needle

4 MEDIUM

Gauge

Gauge is not important for this project.

Pattern Note

Join with slip stitch as indicated unless otherwise stated.

Special Stitch

Single crochet join (sc join): Place slip knot on hook, insert hook in indicated st, yo and draw up a lp, yo and draw through both lps on hook.

Dishcloth

Motif

Make 4.

Row 1 (RS): With red, ch 17, sc in 2nd ch from hook and in each rem ch across, turn. *(16 sc)*

Row 2: Ch 1, sc in each sc across, turn.

Row 3: Rep row 2.

Row 4: Rep row 2, **changing color** *(see Stitch Guide)* to white in last st, turn. Fasten off red.

Rows 5–7: With white, [rep row 2] 3 times.

Row 8: Rep row 2, changing color to red in last st, turn. Fasten off white.

Rows 9–11: With red, [rep row 2] 3 times.

Row 12: Rep row 2, changing color to white in last st, turn. Fasten off red.

Rows 13–16: With white, [rep row 2] 4 times.

At end of row 16, fasten off.

With RS facing, position Motifs in desired pattern and sew tog along adjacent sides.

Edging

Rnd 1: With RS facing, **sc join** *(see Special Stitch)* green in any st or row end, sc evenly around entire piece, working 3 sc in each corner, **join** *(see Pattern Note)* in first sc. Fasten off. ●

Holiday Hexagon

Design by Carol Ballard

Skill Level

 EASY

Finished Measurement

11 inches point to point

Materials

- Medium (worsted) weight cotton yarn:
    1½ oz/75 yds/45g each red and red/white/green variegated
- Size H/8/5mm crochet hook or size needed to obtain gauge
- Tapestry needle

Gauge

7 dc = 2 inches; 3 dc rows = 2 inches

Take time to check gauge.

Pattern Notes

Join with slip stitch as indicated unless otherwise stated.

Chain-3 at beginning of round counts as first double crochet unless otherwise stated.

Chain-4 at beginning of round counts as first double crochet and chain-1 space unless otherwise stated.

Special Stitches

Single crochet join (sc join): Place slip knot on hook, insert hook in indicated st, yo and draw up a lp, yo and draw through both lps on hook.

Picot: Ch 3, sl st in 3rd ch from hook as indicated in instructions.

Dishcloth

Rnd 1 (RS): With red, ch 2, 6 sc in 2nd ch from hook, **join** (see Pattern Notes) in first sc. (6 sc)

Rnd 2: Ch 3 (see Pattern Notes), 2 dc in same st as joining, 3 dc in each rem sc around, join in top of beg ch-3. Fasten off red. (18 dc)

Rnd 3: With RS facing, **sc join** (see Special Stitches) variegated in any dc, ch 3, sk next 2 dc, [sc in next dc, ch 3, sk next 2 dc] around, join in first sc. (6 sc, 6 ch-3 sps)

Rnd 4: Ch 1, sl st in next ch-3 sp, ch 1, (sc, hdc, 3 dc, hdc, sc) in same sp, (sc, hdc, 3 dc, hdc, sc) in each rem ch-3 sp around, join in first sc. Fasten off variegated.

Rnd 5: With RS facing, sc join red in center dc of any 3-dc group, 7 dc in sp between next 2 sc, [sc in center dc of next 3-dc group, 7 dc in sp between next 2 sc] around, join in first sc.

Rnd 6: Ch 1, sc in same st as joining, dc in next dc, [ch 1, dc in next dc] 6 times, *sc in next sc, dc in next dc, [ch 1, dc in next dc] 6 times, rep from * around, join in first sc. Fasten off red.

Rnd 7: With RS facing, join variegated in any sc, ch 3, [dc in next dc, dc in next ch-1 sp] 3 times, (dc, ch 1, dc) in next dc, [dc in next ch-1 sp, dc in next dc] 3 times, *dc in next sc, [dc in next dc, dc in next ch-1 sp] 3 times, (dc, ch 1, dc) in next dc, [dc in next ch-1 sp, dc in next dc] 3 times, rep from * around, join in top of beg ch-3. Fasten off variegated.

Rnd 8: With RS facing, join red in any corner ch-1 sp, **ch 4** *(see Pattern Notes)*, dc in same sp, dc in each of next 15 dc, [(dc, ch 1, dc) in next ch-1 sp, dc in each of next 15 dc] around, join in 3rd ch of beg ch-4. Fasten off red.

Rnd 9: With RS facing, sc join variegated in any ch-1 sp, (**picot**—*see Special Stitches*, sc) in same sp, sc in each rem dc around, working (sc, picot, sc) in each corner ch-1 sp, join in first sc. Fasten off variegated. ●

Scrubby

Design by Maggie Weldon

Skill Level
 EASY

Finished Measurement
9 inches in diameter

Materials
- Medium (worsted) weight cotton yarn:
  1½ oz/75 yds/45g white fleck
  ½ oz/25 yds/15g blue
- Size H/8/5mm crochet hook
- Tapestry needle
- 3-inch diameter plastic mesh pot scrubber

4 MEDIUM

Gauge
Gauge is not important for this project.

Pattern Notes
Join with slip stitch as indicated unless otherwise stated.

Chain-4 at beginning of round counts as first half double crochet and chain-2 space unless otherwise stated.

Dishcloth
Rnd 1 (RS): With white, leaving 12-inch end, ch 36, sl st in first ch to form ring, taking care not to twist ch, ch 1, 2 dc in first ch, dc in next 2 chs, [2 dc in next ch,

dc in next 2 chs] around, **join** (see Pattern Notes) in first dc. (48 dc)

Rnd 2: Ch 1, 2 dc in first dc, dc in next 3 dc, [2 dc in next dc, dc in next 3 dc] around, join in first dc. Fasten off. (60 dc)

Rnd 3: With RS facing, join blue in any dc, **ch 4** (see Pattern Notes), sk next dc, [hdc in next dc, ch 2, sk next dc] around, join in 2nd ch of beg ch-4. Fasten off. (30 hdc, 30 ch-1 sps)

Rnd 4: With RS facing, join white in any ch-2 sp, ch 1, 3 dc in same sp, 3 dc in each rem ch-2 sp around, join in first dc. (90 dc)

Rnd 5: Ch 1, 2 dc in first dc, dc in each of next 8 dc, [2 dc in next dc, dc in each of next 8 dc] around, join in first dc. Fasten off. (100 dc)

Finishing

Using long end on foundation ch, sew scrubber to inside of rnd 1. ●

Christmas Lace

Design by Carol Showers

Skill Level

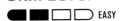 EASY

Finished Measurement

9½ inches in diameter

Materials

- Medium (worsted) weight cotton yarn:
    1 oz/50 yds/30g each red and white fleck
- Size I/9/5.5mm crochet hook
- Tapestry needle

4 MEDIUM

Gauge

Gauge is not important for this project.

Pattern Notes

Join with slip stitch as indicated unless otherwise stated.

Chain-2 at beginning of round does not count as a stitch unless otherwise stated.

Special Stitch

Shell: (Sc, ch 3, sc) in indicated st or sp.

Dishcloth

Rnd 1 (RS): With red, ch 4, 11 dc in 4th ch from hook (sk chs count as first dc), **join** (see Pattern Notes) in 3rd ch of beg ch-4. (12 dc)

Rnd 2: Ch 2 *(see Pattern Notes)*, 2 dc in first st, 2 dc in each rem dc around, join in first dc. *(24 dc)*

Rnd 3: Ch 2, dc in first st, 2 dc in next dc, [dc in next dc, 2 dc in next dc] 11 times, join in first dc. *(36 dc)*

Rnd 4: Ch 2, dc in first dc, [2 dc in next dc] twice, *dc in next dc, [2 dc in next dc] twice, rep from * around, join in first dc. *(60 dc)*

Rnd 5: Ch 2, dc in first dc, dc in each of next 3 dc, 2 dc in next dc, [dc in each of next 4 dc, 2 dc in next dc] 11 times, **changing color** *(see Stitch Guide)* to white fleck in last st, join in first dc. Fasten off red. *(72 dc)*

Rnd 6: Ch 1, **shell** *(see Special Stitch)* in first dc, sk next dc, [shell in next dc, skip next dc] around, join in first sc. *(36 shells)*

Rnds 7 & 8: Sl st in next ch-3 sp, ch 1, shell in same sp, shell in ch-3 sp of each rem shell around, join in first sc.

At end last rnd, fasten off. ●

STITCH GUIDE

STITCH ABBREVIATIONS

beg	begin/begins/beginning
bpdc	back post double crochet
bpsc	back post single crochet
bptr	back post treble crochet
CC	contrasting color
ch(s)	chain(s)
ch-	refers to chain or space previously made (i.e., ch-1 space)
ch sp(s)	chain space(s)
cl(s)	cluster(s)
cm	centimeter(s)
dc	double crochet (singular/plural)
dc dec	double crochet 2 or more stitches together, as indicated
dec	decrease/decreases/decreasing
dtr	double treble crochet
ext	extended
fpdc	front post double crochet
fpsc	front post single crochet
fptr	front post treble crochet
g	gram(s)
hdc	half double crochet
hdc dec	half double crochet 2 or more stitches together, as indicated
inc	increase/increases/increasing
lp(s)	loop(s)
MC	main color
mm	millimeter(s)
oz	ounce(s)
pc	popcorn(s)
rem	remain/remains/remaining
rep(s)	repeat(s)
rnd(s)	round(s)
RS	right side
sc	single crochet (singular/plural)
sc dec	single crochet 2 or more stitches together, as indicated
sk	skip/skipped/skipping
sl st(s)	slip stitch(es)
sp(s)	space(s)/spaced
st(s)	stitch(es)
tog	together
tr	treble crochet
trtr	triple treble
WS	wrong side
yd(s)	yard(s)
yo	yarn over

YARN CONVERSION

OUNCES TO GRAMS		GRAMS TO OUNCES	
1	28.4	25	⅞
2	56.7	40	1⅔
3	85.0	50	1¾
4	113.4	100	3½

UNITED STATES		UNITED KINGDOM
sl st (slip stitch)	=	sc (single crochet)
sc (single crochet)	=	dc (double crochet)
hdc (half double crochet)	=	htr (half treble crochet)
dc (double crochet)	=	tr (treble crochet)
tr (treble crochet)	=	dtr (double treble crochet)
dtr (double treble crochet)	=	ttr (triple treble crochet)
skip	=	miss

Single crochet decrease (sc dec): (Insert hook, yo, draw lp through) in each of the sts indicated, yo, draw through all lps on hook.

Example of 2-sc dec

Half double crochet decrease (hdc dec): (Yo, insert hook, yo, draw lp through) in each of the sts indicated, yo, draw through all lps on hook.

Example of 2-hdc dec

Reverse single crochet (reverse sc): Ch 1, sk first st, working from left to right, insert hook in next st from front to back, draw up lp on hook, yo and draw through both lps on hook.

Chain (ch): Yo, pull through lp on hook.

Single crochet (sc): Insert hook in st, yo, pull through st, yo, pull through both lps on hook.

Double crochet (dc): Yo, insert hook in st, yo, pull through st, [yo, pull through 2 lps] twice.

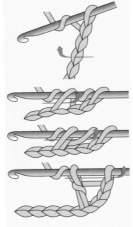

Double crochet decrease (dc dec): (Yo, insert hook, yo, draw lp through, yo, draw through 2 lps on hook) in each of the sts indicated, yo, draw through all lps on hook.

Example of 2-dc dec

Front loop (front lp) Back loop (back lp)

Front Loop   Back Loop

Front post stitch (fp): Back post stitch (bp): When working post st, insert hook from right to left around post of st on previous row.

Back   Front

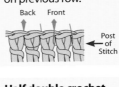

Post of Stitch

Half double crochet (hdc): Yo, insert hook in st, yo, pull through st, yo, pull through all 3 lps on hook.

Double treble crochet (dtr): Yo 3 times, insert hook in st, yo, pull through st, [yo, pull through 2 lps] 4 times.

Treble crochet decrease (tr dec): Holding back last lp of each st, tr in each of the sts indicated, yo, pull through all lps on hook.

Example of 2-tr dec

Slip stitch (sl st): Insert hook in st, pull through both lps on hook.

Chain color change (ch color change) Yo with new color, draw through last lp on hook.

Double crochet color change (dc color change) Drop first color, yo with new color, draw through last 2 lps of st.

Treble crochet (tr): Yo twice, insert hook in st, yo, pull through st, [yo, pull through 2 lps] 3 times.

Metric Conversion Charts

METRIC CONVERSIONS				
yards	x	.9144	=	metres (m)
yards	x	91.44	=	centimetres (cm)
inches	x	2.54	=	centimetres (cm)
inches	x	25.40	=	millimetres (mm)
inches	x	.0254	=	metres (m)

centimetres	x	.3937	=	inches
metres	x	1.0936	=	yards

INCHES INTO MILLIMETRES & CENTIMETRES (Rounded off slightly)

inches	mm	cm	inches	cm	inches	cm	inches	cm
1/8	3	0.3	5	12.5	21	53.5	38	96.5
1/4	6	0.6	5 1/2	14	22	56	39	99
3/8	10	1	6	15	23	58.5	40	101.5
1/2	13	1.3	7	18	24	61	41	104
5/8	15	1.5	8	20.5	25	63.5	42	106.5
3/4	20	2	9	23	26	66	43	109
7/8	22	2.2	10	25.5	27	68.5	44	112
1	25	2.5	11	28	28	71	45	114.5
1 1/4	32	3.2	12	30.5	29	73.5	46	117
1 1/2	38	3.8	13	33	30	76	47	119.5
1 3/4	45	4.5	14	35.5	31	79	48	122
2	50	5	15	38	32	81.5	49	124.5
2 1/2	65	6.5	16	40.5	33	84	50	127
3	75	7.5	17	43	34	86.5		
3 1/2	90	9	18	46	35	89		
4	100	10	19	48.5	36	91.5		
4 1/2	115	11.5	20	51	37	94		

KNITTING NEEDLES CONVERSION CHART

Canada/U.S.	0	1	2	3	4	5	6	7	8	9	10	10½	11	13	15
Metric (mm)	2	2¼	2¾	3¼	3½	3¾	4	4½	5	5½	6	6½	8	9	10

CROCHET HOOKS CONVERSION CHART

Canada/U.S.	1/B	2/C	3/D	4/E	5/F	6/G	8/H	9/I	10/J	10½/K	N
Metric (mm)	2.25	2.75	3.25	3.5	3.75	4.25	5	5.5	6	6.5	9.0

Annie's®

A Year of Dishcloths is published by Annie's, 306 East Parr Road, Berne, IN 46711. Printed in USA. Copyright © 2016, 2017 Annie's. All rights reserved. This publication may not be reproduced in part or in whole without written permission from the publisher.

RETAIL STORES: If you would like to carry this publication or any other Annie's publication, visit AnniesWSL.com.

Every effort has been made to ensure that the instructions in this publication are complete and accurate. We cannot, however, take responsibility for human error, typographical mistakes or variations in individual work. Please visit AnniesCustomerService.com to check for pattern updates.

ISBN: 978-1-59012-314-0   Library of Congress Control Number: 2015959448   7 8 9